911

THE BOOK OF HELP

EDITED BY MICHAEL CART

WITH MARC ARONSON AND MARIANNE CARUS

CRICKET BOOKS
A Marcato Book
CHICAGO

Library of Congress Cataloging-in-Publication Data

911 : the book of help / edited by Michael Cart ; with Marianne Carus
and Marc Aronson.— 1st ed.
    p. cm.
"A Marcato Book."
Summary: A collection of essays, poems, short fiction, and drawings
created in response to the terrorist attacks of September 11, 2001, by
authors and illustrators of books for young adults.
    ISBN 0-8126-2659-1 (cloth : alk. paper) — ISBN 0-8126-2676-1 (pbk. :
alk. paper)
    1. September 11 Terrorist Attacks, 2001—Literary collections. 2.
Terrorism—Literary collections. [1. September 11 Terrorist Attacks,
2001—Literary collections. 2. Terrorism—Literary collections.] I.
Title: Nine-one-one. II. Cart, Michael. III. Carus, Marianne. IV.
Aronson, Marc.
    PZ5 .A17 2002
    810.8'0358—dc21
                                                        2002004707

CONTENTS

ACKNOWLEDGMENTS

We at Carus Publishing owe many debts of gratitude to members of the publishing community for their contributions to this book. First and foremost, all of the authors and artists who appear here gave generously of their time and talent, often through many revisions, even though the only compensation they received was the opportunity to respond to the tragedy and to give something to the victims. Other creators, equally eager to be of help, sent us work that we were unable to use. Even though their names are not in the table of contents, they played important parts in shaping the book. Michael Cart contributed his understanding and knowledge long before his words. Our colleagues in other publishing houses were always ready to supply suggestions and contact information, and became in that way collaborators in the work. Judy O'Malley took care of the thousand details that made this book a reality. We are grateful to Pat Scales for creating the Teacher's Guide, which extends the reach of this book by making it more useful for classes. Special thanks to Robie Harris and Nicole Hollander, who collaborated to create a dynamic graphic short story, which we hope will make it easier for young

people to begin talking, or not talking, about It. Their work appears in the Guide. Our thanks go, too, to Dr. Donna Gaffney, coordinator of the Traumatic Loss Coalition in Essex County, New Jersey, for creating a guide for parents and mental health professionals who wish to share this book with young adults.

The spirit of generosity that characterized the creation of the book continued once it moved on from manuscript to print. Maple-Vail Book Manufacturing Group and Pinnacle Press, Inc., and our distributor, Publishers Group West, offered to do their work at or below cost so we would be able to pass along more money to the Families of Freedom Scholarship Fund.

Finally, the inspiration for this book came in the days just after the attack when so many of us wanted to volunteer, to give something, and had nothing the victims or those aiding them needed. The crucial first step that made the book seem possible came in a series of calls with Valerie Lewis of the excellent children's bookstore Hicklebee's. Her enthusiasm, her contacts, and her conviction gave the project momentum that has carried through to this day. Thank you, to all of you.

Marc Aronson
Marianne Carus

INTRODUCTION

I was born on March 6, 1941, seven months and one day before the surprise attack on Pearl Harbor, a day of unspeakable death and destruction that President Franklin Roosevelt declared would "live in infamy."

Since we humans often struggle to make sense of the senseless by citing analogous events from history, December 7 would often be invoked in the immediate aftermath of the horrors of September 11, 2001, another infamous day of death and destruction. And, in fact, the words "Pearl Harbor" were among the first to flash into my own mind as I became aware of what was happening in New York, Washington, D.C., and rural Pennsylvania. The words personally connected me to what was occurring, and I was stunned to think that my life, which began in a year of infamy, might end in another year of infamy, for I'm sure I'm not the only American to have wondered, however fleetingly, if the terror by airplane were only the beginning of a more universal cataclysm.

For America, it seemed, was under attack, and the taken-for-granted security of living in a country separated from the rest of the world by two vast oceans vanished in the instant of the first plane's impact.

In my life, I have lived through a number of wars—or, as they are sometimes cosmetically called, "conflicts," "crises," "police actions," "incursions," and even "nation buildings." Too young in 1941 to remember Pearl Harbor, my memory of this kind of large-scale violence begins with the Korean War when I was nine, though even that was something happening "over there" in a remote country I had never before heard of.

The Cuban missile crisis of October 1962 struck closer to the home of my personal consciousness, since I was then a junior in college. And I remember standing in a pharmacy two blocks from campus, listening, transfixed, to a radio newscast. It sounded as if war were imminent and I remember thinking, with a sinking feeling, that my life might be over, since I and others of my generation would likely be the first to be sent into harm's way. This was a deeply disquieting thought and one that seldom strayed far from my consciousness as world conflict shifted to Vietnam, and I—still eminently draftable—went off to graduate school. In fact, I would eventually wind up serving in the U.S. Army during that war in Southeast Asia, but, mercifully, the closest I came to seeing action was through writing "after-action reports" from my snug haven as a military historian stationed in Thailand.

Accordingly, in the wake of 9/11, what made the opening salvos of what is being called a "war on terrorism" so different to me was that the continental United States was actually under attack for the first time in my life. For all I knew, there at the outset, friends of mine in New York were in terrible jeopardy simply because of where they lived. Indeed, the first I heard about the unfolding events was an instant message I received while I was on-line, reading my early morning e-mail. It came from a writer friend in Brooklyn who wrote, "I'm cowering in terror in my apartment."

"What are you talking about?" I typed in reply.

"A plane just flew into the World Trade Center," she answered. "They think it's a terrorist attack."

My response to that was to rush to the TV and to watch, unbelieving, as a second plane flew into the first tower's twin.

How to describe what I felt? At first, it was numbness and incomprehension—my brain couldn't understand what my eyes were seeing. It was only as the words of the newscasters began to penetrate my consciousness that the images came into a kind of bewildered focus. And I suddenly felt an imperative need to talk about this thing that was transpiring, so I called my family in Indiana and my friends here in California. We were, we cautiously agreed, "all right," but underlying our words was a clear uncertainty about the future, a sense of waiting for what might happen next.

I returned to the television and watched the twin towers collapse into rubble, saw smoke billow from a gaping wound in the face of the Pentagon, observed people run from the White House, and peered at a patch of Pennsylvania countryside where a jet plane—perhaps bound for Washington to do further damage— had crashed.

I watched and felt empty—no, I felt helpless, out of control, and at the mercy of faceless others who, it seemed, were not at all kindly disposed toward me and other Americans.

I had the nagging sense that I had felt this way once before, but the memory of when it might have been was tanta-lizingly elusive. In the days that followed, that memory remained fugitive, crowded further into obscurity by other more immediate feelings: anger born of frustration, guilt at being a survivor, and—though I'm reluctant to admit it, since I consider myself a person of good will—moments of hatred for those who had perpetrated these atrocities.

I also felt an urgent need to do something—but what could I do? Since a continent separated me from serving as a vol-unteer at ground zero, all I could do was express my concern for my friends in New York and make a donation to one of the sev-eral survivor funds that sprang into being. It didn't seem to be enough, and so I rejoiced at the opportunity that was soon offered to participate in the making of this book. Here was something I could do, since words are my work.

I was also eager to read what words the distinguished contributors to this collection might express about the events of 9/11 and their aftermath, since I was anxious to learn from their reactions and reflections how I might come to think about the unthinkable.

Reading the essays, stories, and poems as they arrived, I began reflecting on what words of my own I might use for this introduction. And suddenly I remembered when it was that I had felt exactly as I felt the morning of September 11: it had been another morning, January 4, 1994, when, at 4:31, I had been awakened by a violent shaking that I realized, instantly, was an earthquake, but one unlike any of the many others I had previously experienced during two decades of living in Los Angeles. For I had never before been convinced I was going to die. It wasn't only the violence of the shaking or the stygian blackness (because of ambient light, it's never really dark in L.A., even at 4:31 in the morning, but this quake had knocked out all electric power); it was the fact that I was living on the tenth floor of a twelve-story apartment building and the infernal crashing noises I was hearing as I shook in my bed like a pea in a pan were the sounds of the building collapsing around me.

I remember being surprised that this was how I was going to die and I remember being even more surprised that I was, in fact, going to die. Had I secretly thought myself immortal? Perhaps, for I felt a momentary pang of regret about my mortality as I lay there, helplessly waiting for the building to collapse. Then, reflexively, I did what I had been taught to do as a little boy when I had been taken by my mother, week in and week out, to Sunday school and church: I closed my eyes against the darkness and uttered a prayer, asking for God's forgiveness and entrance into heaven.

Well, I didn't die, of course. The shaking finally subsided and I discovered, when I tried to get out of bed to escape my apartment, that the crashing had not, after all, been the building falling down, but, rather, the sound of twenty-three of the twenty-four six-foot-tall bookcases that lined the walls of my large apartment falling to the floor and sending the 6,000 books they contained flying to every remote corner.

Several hours later, when daylight finally dawned and I was permitted back into my apartment, I was bemused to discover that one solitary bookcase remained standing. What books did it contain? My large collection of books about angels.

What am I to make of this? Reflecting on those two mornings now, I find it strange but trivial. Others, however, might find an important message in it—for I did survive, after all, and maybe not by accident but by design.

But if that is so, what about the fifty-seven who did not survive that earthquake or the thousands who, seven years later, did not survive the events of 9/11? Was that accident . . . or design?

I am left wondering what to believe.

And I wonder if future historians will record that these two seismic events—so linked in my own mind—caused a sea change in the way succeeding generations would think about the world and their existence in it. Might these events, by inviting people to examine their most cherished beliefs, usher in a new age of faith or might they—as another cataclysm, the horrific 1755 Lisbon earthquake did—help spur a new age of reason?

Who knows? As for me, I remain uncertain what to think or believe—except to continue, passionately and stubbornly, to think that words are important and to believe in their saving power, in their power to inform the mind, heal the spirit, and help us deal with even the worst of adversity.

And that, after all, is the reason for this book. We editors have asked a number of our favorite writers to reflect on September 11, confident that their candid and heartfelt reactions will help readers to process and come to terms with the events of that awful time.

The writers responded, as we hoped they would, in a variety of ways: some celebrated the heroes of 9/11 and its aftermath; others provided a record of events and historic context for the day; while still others grappled with their own deepest feelings to provide an emotional road map for catharsis and individual recovery. There are stories, personal essays, and poems, which embrace all aspects of a day that touched every single one of our lives.

One of the awful ironies of the attacks is that they occurred on a date, 9/11, that is the same as the telephone number we are accustomed to call for emergency assistance. By calling this book *911: The Book of Help*, we hope to underscore the fact that 911 must remain not only a telephone number but also a symbol of the selfless human capacity to aid those in every sort of need.

And as I express my thanks to the community of authors who have helped by so generously contributing their work and words to this collection, I also express my hope that the community of young adults who read their words will be helped by them to think—and talk—about the otherwise unthinkable and unspeakable. That's how healing begins.

—Michael Cart

HEALING

"No one has been untouched . . ."

HEALING

As the contributions for this collection began arriving, they seemed to fall, naturally, into four thematic sections that we're calling "Healing," "Searching for History," "Asking Why? Why? Why?" and "Reacting and Recovering." Each section is introduced by one of artist Chris Raschka's powerful sketches, done as the second tower fell.

Since healing is uppermost in our minds, we start with that theme, beginning with Katherine Paterson's "Repairing Spirits in Disarray," which coincidentally, was the very first submission to arrive. All of us involved with the collection realized, immediately, that it offered the perfect way to begin the book, since it not only puts events into a global framework, but also dramatically demonstrates how stories have the power to heal wounded spirits everywhere.

Appropriately, the second piece is by Katherine Paterson's son, David Paterson, whose childhood loss of a friend inspired his mother to write her novel *Bridge to Terabithia* as an exercise in emotional healing. Now an adult, David takes readers inside Ground Zero, as he compellingly writes from the midst of the rescue efforts about his experience serving as a volunteer in the immediate wake of the attacks.

Russell Freedman celebrates another kind of heroism and sacrifice in his moving essay about a neighborhood's search for healing through holding a candlelight vigil in honor of New York City firefighters who gave their lives to help others.

Joan Bauer tells a story of the devastating impact of 9/11 on young people, and of how one Brooklyn girl—with the help of a friend—finds healing through recovering her pre–9/11 life and sense of purpose.

And we conclude this section with Sonya Sones's haunting and cathartic poem, which promises a first step to healing by giving voices to some of those who died.

REPAIRING SPIRITS IN DISARRAY

BY KATHERINE PATERSON

Sometimes it seemed to him that his life was delicate as a dandelion.
One little puff from any direction, and it was blown to bits.

—Bridge to Terabithia

In December 1999, I opened my newspaper to read about terrible floods and mud slides in the state of Vargas on the coast of Venezuela. Tens of thousands of people were dead or missing and presumed dead. It is easy to feel helpless in the face of such a monumental tragedy, but I knew at once there was something I could do.

The previous October in honor of my winning the Hans Christian Andersen Prize in 1998, the United States Board on Books for Young People (USBBY) had given me a wonderful gift—$13,000—that I would have the privilege of giving away to another section of the International Board on Books for Young People (IBBY) anywhere in the world. Naturally, I felt a special responsibility to see that the gift was put to worthy use. I asked several people for recommendations, but was still hesitating when I opened my newspaper that morning. I knew immediately that Venezuela was the place to which I wanted to send the gift.

I e-mailed Carmen Diana Dearden, past president of IBBY, who lives in Caracas. Carmen Diana, who is publisher of Ekare Books and chair of the board of Banco del Libro, had been consulting with her colleagues as to what beyond physical necessities they could provide for the devastated survivors of what has become known in Venezuela as "the tragedy." The tragedy occurred when the coastal mountain range, swollen by months of heavy rains, simply collapsed along its river and stream beds, killing anywhere from 30,000 to 100,000 people and leaving many others bereaved and homeless. The money from the USBBY would be used to buy books and book bags for a volunteer project Banco del Libro had envisioned, called Read to Live (*Leer para Vivir*).

Using a four-wheel-drive vehicle to take them over the mountain since the road was impassable, the volunteers first went to a small school in the barrio of Quenepe, near the port of La Guaira. They had sent word that the storytellers were coming, and the frightened, exhausted people of the community came and brought their children for an afternoon of respite. In the midst of the story there was a rumbling sound. Everyone, including the storyteller, froze. Even the fearless Carmen Diana sidled over to the window to see if the mountain was once more collapsing. She assured everyone that it was just a plane taking off from the newly opened airport nearby, and the story continued. Before the afternoon was over, books had been read aloud, games had been played, and the volunteers and people of the community were singing together. Afterward two parents came up and asked to borrow books. It hadn't been a part of the original plan, but the volunteers said, "Of course." And those two parents, one a mother, the other a father, took the books home, gathered their family and neighbors, and began to have story time in their own homes.

On my way to the IBBY Congress in Cartagena, Colombia, in September 2000, I went to Venezuela to see first-hand some of the work of the Read to Live program which the gift from USBBY had helped to fund. The scars were still visible on the mountain, though the fast-growing greenery of the tropics was beginning to cover them. "At first," says Carmen Diana, "it looked as though a giant tiger had scratched the mountainside." The great gullies that marked the paths of the destruction remained. In them were the huge boulders that the floods and mud slides had brought down. Thousands of bodies remained buried beneath the rocks and dried mud. Tens of thousands of the living remained homeless. Children had lost parents, and parents children. No one was untouched.

School was on vacation, so we met in Jennifer's house across from the school in Quenepe where the initial session of Read to Live was held. Gathered in Jennifer's living room were those first parents who came and who now had made for them-selves lovely yellow banners (to match the yellow book bags) announcing that their homes were Read to Live homes where their neighbors could come for storytelling and reading. "Tell them your anecdote, Nancy," someone said. "I work," said Nancy, "with children who are very disturbed. Most of them have to be on medication. Recently I decided to read to them *Willy the Dreamer* [by the 2000 Andersen Award winner Anthony

Browne]. Afterward one of the most troubled and troublesome boys came up to me. 'You don't have to give me any more medicine,' he said. 'I'm going to be like Willy the Dreamer.' He hasn't had any more medicine since that time," Nancy said. "And he's doing OK."

As my part of the sharing, I told the parents in Jennifer's living room the story of how I had come to write *Bridge to Terabithia*, a book of mine that Carmen Diana had read to them as they were being trained to be leaders of the Read to Live program.

In the spring of 1974, I told them, with Carmen Diana translating, I learned that I had cancer—a very ordinary, garden variety of the disease—which was found early, operated upon, and has not in these past twenty-six years ever troubled me again. But at the time it didn't seem so ordinary to me. I had four young children. The thought of dying at all was frightening, but the thought of leaving my children seemed more than I could bear.

The year had already been a hard one for the children. The small school they attended was closed, and they were sent to a much larger school on the other side of town. David, our second grader, was miserable. Then one day the funny, happy little boy that I thought I'd lost forever came running in from school. "Me and Lisa Hill are making a diorama of *Little House in the Big Woods!*" he cried, beaming all over. I'd never heard of Lisa Hill until that moment. From then on I was to hear hardly any other name.

Lisa was a wonderful friend. She was bright, joy-filled, a natural athlete. She laughed at David's jokes (the ones his older brother and sister groaned over), and he laughed at hers. They played long, imaginative games in the woods behind her house, and in the late spring they both turned eight years old.

On a bright August afternoon, the phone call came. I listened in disbelief and horror and then quickly bypassed David, reading in the living room, to search out his father. Lisa was dead. Killed by lightning on a bright summer afternoon.

"I know why Lisa died," he said one night after his prayers. "It's because God hates me. Probably he's going to kill Mary next." (Mary is his beloved younger sister.)

David decided that God had made a list and was going to kill off everyone he loved. Indeed, his cherished third-grade teacher told me afterward that she had had a miscarriage that winter. When a substitute teacher appeared and David learned Mrs. Beckman was in the hospital, he ran away from school and was persuaded to return only when the principal went out and found him hiding in a tree in the park nearby and promised him he'd had nothing to do with his teacher's mishap. Every time my husband or I left the house, David was sure we would never return.

In January I went to the regular monthly meeting of the Children's Book Guild of Washington, D.C. We members took turns sitting at the head table with the guest speaker for the luncheon, and it happened to be my turn. I had never met the speaker before. She was the senior editor for a New York publishing house. In the quiet chitchat before the meal was served, one of my fellow members said to me quite innocently, "How are the children?" I opened my mouth to say "Fine, thank you," and what came spewing out was a stream of anguish. In the rational part of my mind, I knew I was behaving badly, but I couldn't help myself. The story of my son's pain simply poured out.

I couldn't stop, but finally, I ran out. There was a long silence. And then the guest of honor from New York said gently, "I know this sounds just like an editor, but you ought to write that story."

I went home that day and thought about what the editor had said. I couldn't do what I wanted to do. I wanted to bring back Lisa from the dead. I couldn't even comfort my grieving child. So I would do what I could. I would write a story that would somehow help me make sense of this senseless tragedy.

The book was moving forward, going well, until suddenly, one day I realized that when I began work the next day I would be writing the chapter in which the little girl would die. I solved that problem. I just didn't go to work the next day. I straightened my shelves. I did the laundry. I even cleaned the kitchen. That took several days. I was reduced to scrubbing the floors on my hands and knees when a longtime friend of mine asked quite casually, "How is your book going?"

She of course didn't know what book I was writing, or even that no one is ever supposed to ask me how my work is going. But we have been friends since school days and she feels free to say anything she wants to me.

So I did what I had done months before at the luncheon. I blubbered out the truth. I told her the book was terrible and going nowhere. "I guess," I said, thinking I was very wise, "I guess I just can't go through Lisa's death again."

Estelle looked me straight in the eye. "I don't think it's Lisa's death you can't face, Katherine. I think it's yours."

I went home to my study and shut the door. If it were Lisa's death I couldn't face that was one thing, but if it were my own, there was no escape. I would have to finish the book. I wrote the chapter and moved straight through to the end of the draft, the sweat pouring down my arms. And because I could not stand to have it around, I did what no professional writer would ever do: I mailed the manuscript to my editor, Virginia Buckley, before the sweat had evaporated.

As soon as I left the post office, I was seized with terror. What had I done? What would my editor think of this terrible book? Finally, Virginia called. "I want to talk to you about this new manuscript." "Yes." "I laughed through the first two thirds and cried through the last," she said. I nearly collapsed with relief. "Now," she said, "let's turn it into a book."

I love revisions. As I've often said, revisions are the only place in life where you can take spilt milk and turn it into ice cream. The initial writing of *Bridge to Terabithia* had been one of the worst experiences of my life. The rewriting was one of the most glorious.

I was so elated that I wrote to Virginia: "I know that love is blind because I've just mailed you a flawless manuscript."

You'll be happy to know that my sight was soon restored. I knew perfectly well that it was not a flawless manuscript anymore than a child of mine is without sin. But I loved it almost as fiercely. I didn't think the world would. But in a funny way, I didn't care. The book had done so much for me that I couldn't be bothered about critics or the general public. If I thought about reactions to the book at all, I thought that probably no one whose name was not Paterson would be able to understand it.

The book will be twenty-five years old in 2002. It has sold literally millions of copies in more than twenty-five languages. I suppose I can no longer maintain that you have to be named Paterson to understand it. But as my friends in Venezuela proved once again, readers have brought to this book their own lives— joys, pains, sorrows—and the gift of their own imaginations, and have made this simple little story into something far more wonderful than I could have ever made it alone.

Banco del Libro had originally planned to train teachers in the state of Vargas, and they did. But they had also trained the parents I met in Jennifer's living room. Team coordinator Carmen

Martinez and her group met with these first parents once a week for five months. As part of the training each week, Carmen Diana Dearden decided to read aloud *Bridge to Terabithia*. When she got to the place in the story when it begins to rain, she could feel the tension mounting in the room. "Shall I stop reading?" she asked. "Yes." There was a pause, then, "No. Go on." She read to the end of the book that afternoon. "Everyone was crying, including me," she said. And then the mother they called "Shy Maria" to distinguish her from the other Maria said quietly, "I think this means that we must begin to build our own new bridges."

And build them they did. Carmen Diana told me recently that there are now sixty-two lending centers in four communities in the state of Vargas. The local leaders are teachers and parents, some of whom went back to school to learn how to read well enough to share books with their children and neighbors. People whose only reading in the past was the occasional newspaper or magazine are not only discovering the joy of books, but are sharing that love with their families and neighbors. One participant told Carmen Martinez, "Everything is so terrible after the tragedy, but now I know when I need peace, I can open a book and begin to read."

Since September 11, 2001, we in the United States have now some taste of the fear and suffering that our brothers and sisters in other nations have known for many years. And yet, expressions of sympathy have been pouring in from people and places whose pain has gone on for decades. Many Americans have been deeply touched by the expressions of sorrow that have come to us from all over the world during this difficult time. We feel a new kinship with the rest of the world that many in the United States have never experienced before.

My times in other countries have taught me a great deal about the injustice we Americans have knowingly or unknowingly inflicted on other peoples. I hope through our own national distress, the leaders of our government and our people as a whole will open our eyes and ears and hearts to what the rest of the world is saying to us.

During these dark days many of us have turned as never before to the arts. The essayist Barry Lopez says that the task of fiction is to "sustain us with illumination and heal us . . . to repair a spirit in disarray." I believe this is the task of all of the arts—of literature, music, dance, theater, the graphic arts—to sustain us with illumination, to heal us, to repair our devastated spirits. Art takes the pain and chaos of our broken world and transforms it into something that brings forth life.

As for the terrors ahead—for he did not fool himself that they were all behind him—well, you just have to stand up to your fear and not let it squeeze you white. Right, Leslie?

Right.

—Bridge to Terabithia

THE DECISION TO GO

BY DAVID PATERSON

"We swept up a lot of people today. . . ." I was into my seventh hour of a sixteen-hour day at the base of what remained of the World Trade Center complex. Ronnie, a front-end loader operator who worked for New York City Transit, noted the confusion on my face. "When they went down, the combination of friction, existing fires, and remaining jet fuel created a blast furnace effect that incinerated everything in the nearby blocks . . . there were a lot of people down here—watching, thinking they were safe. They're not here anymore." The rest of our crew nodded in silent agreement. Nothing more needed to be said.

I awoke at 4:20 Thursday morning to the cries of my nineteen-month-old. After giving him his bottle, I could not go back to bed. I turned on the television. The World Trade Center had been bombed forty-four hours earlier and chaos remained the

13

order of the day. I'm not sure what exactly was going through my head, but frustration was one of the stronger emotions guiding my decision. I went to the basement and dug out my old hard hat from my construction years. I collected my belt clip, tin snips, goggles, dust masks, flashlight, my Timberland boots, and a few other tools before heading off to the train station in Manhasset, New York. I caught the 5:09 into Manhattan. I didn't wake my wife, Ariana.

The train had a surprising number of people. As a stay-at-home father of two, I had never taken the train at that hour, but I understand it can be quite full. The conductor passed through collecting tickets. He saw my gear before seeing my face and quietly passed by, not stopping to take my outstretched ticket. He knew where I was going.

At Penn Station, I passed several officers who looked into my eyes and said nothing, but they knew where I was going. I caught the A-train to Fourteenth Street, as that was as far as trains were allowed to run. As I climbed the stairs, it was still dark, and the acrid taste of smoke hung in the air. I headed south.

My plan was crude at best, but I felt I should try. The day before, I had been drilling into the concrete wall in my basement to install a dryer vent. I had collected the dust and put it in my pockets when I'd left that morning. A few blocks before I reached the barricades, I pulled out the dust and smeared my shirt, shoes, and face with it, to make it appear that I had already been downtown. A lone officer stood at the barricade checking local residents for IDs before letting them pass. He looked up and before he could ask me, I stated, "Demo" (short for demolition) and never broke my stride. The officer stepped aside, "Demo, okay."

I was through. Twenty blocks to go. I passed several other cross-street roadblocks manned by police and soldiers, but was never challenged. The smell of smoke increased, block by block, and I noted that the fine layer of dust on the street was gradually increasing in depth. Several bodegas were open, but it was still early, so few people were on the street. In the distance I could see the heavy white smoke rising and filling the sky.

I called Ariana's office, as I knew she'd check messages, even though she had stayed home, as her office was above Penn Station, and that building was still considered a potential terrorist target. I explained that I had decided to come down to see if I could help. I knew she wanted me home and was probably furious with me, but I hoped she'd understand.

My cell phone lost its signal. There was a steadily increasing haze. I put on my mask. Slowly, through the haze, it began to take shape: the smoking remains of 7 World Trade Center. There were no street signs that I could see—most had been ripped off by the blast. Soldiers, police, firemen, and city workers stood on the corner staring at a group of men surrounding another individual in a full, white hazardous-materials outfit, looking like one of those characters from the movie *Outbreak*.

The haz-mat guy was wrestling with several blueprints and schematics. I asked a man next to me what was going on. He only shrugged. We waited. To avoid boredom we looked at papers driven by the force of the blast into a row of public telephones. The guy to my left pulled out a canceled check for one and a half million dollars from a bank that no longer was there.

Finally, the haz-mat guy pointed down to a section of the street and two men began digging through the debris. I walked over and helped pull aside an abandoned fire hose as a Con Ed truck pulled up. I soon learned that they were trying to find a gas line shutoff valve that was feeding gas into the burning structure below. I helped off-load several pieces of equipment, and I asked one of the Con Ed workers—a woman, but I only knew this when she spoke to me, because she was completely enshrouded in a haz-mat suit—if I could borrow a reflective vest, which she gave me without question. Conversation was kept to a minimum, as people were still trying to take in the enormity of the disaster.

Angry is the best way I can describe the wreckage. Jagged, with towering sections thrusting toward the sky, as if in a vain attempt to rise again. Smoke billowed out from crevices through the collapsed sections of number seven. This one was abandoned before it collapsed, I was told, so there shouldn't be any bodies in there. But "shouldn't" was the strongest confirmation anyone could state.

With the gas line capped and the Con Ed crew heading off to another shutoff valve, I decided to head on to see if I could help out anywhere else. I passed the rows of burned-out emergency vehicles, fire trucks, and postal carriers that lined the ash-covered streets. I found myself on the corner of Church and Vesey, where a hundred or so men were attempting to clean the streets. I grabbed a shovel and helped scoop the dust and small debris into piles collected by junior-sized bulldozers that emptied into larger front-end loaders, which then emptied into dump trucks to take out the debris via the West Side highway.

A swaggering, dark-skinned Portuguese man with a thick cigar hopped down from his giant front-end loader and asked my name. "Today, we are a team, you and me, David. We work together." He asked me if I were Portuguese. I lied. I said, "A little." He winked and told me he could spot a Portuguese from a mile away. He was from Madeira—did I know of it? I knew the wine, which made him smile.

For the next few hours we worked together. I would clear debris from around hydrants and remaining stumps of light posts and street signs, pushing it into the street, where Dennis would scoop it up and deliver it to the trucks. I will never forget the hoses. Hoses from somewhere heading to nowhere. And they were everywhere, stretching from around the burned hulks of the blackened fire trucks of the first reserve teams to the site. The teams who were no more. I found the first use for my tin snips. With some coaxing, they could cut through the rubber and nylon lines. Such a waste, I thought, as I cut through the mass of hoses . . . over a mile of hoses . . . over sixty rescue vehicles . . . over three hundred firemen. The FBI asked us to lift several of the fire trucks with the front-end loaders, so they could look for remains. They found only ash. We were constantly waiting for permission to proceed with cleanup. They needed to look for evidence. "What evidence?" complained one driver. "Two planes hit the World Trade Center—it seems pretty evident." We just wanted to help clean up and clear out. We were forgetting that it was a crime scene.

Among the debris of pulverized concrete and ash and metal were calculators, compacts, laptop computers, toys, and trinkets. I even found a 1000-yen note, which I gave to a passing FBI agent, who thanked me and went on her way.

But what really haunted me were the business cards, thousands of them, each with a different name, but all with the same addresses, 1 Trade Center, 2 Trade Center, 5 Trade Center and so on . . .

As I shoveled, I suddenly saw a small patch of color in the debris. I pulled out and dusted off a 2-inch by 3-inch oil painting of a three-masted schooner on a windswept ocean. A small steel shaft was sticking through the canvas. As I pulled out the shrapnel from the canvas, I noticed, written on the back of the painting, "Seascape study with ship at sea, Sept. 1999" and, at the bottom, the name Sylvia L. Beckey was printed above her signature, and below that, "USA." I stared at the picture, hoping that one day I could get this back to its owner, or if they were no longer alive, maybe Sylvia would want it back. I slipped the painting into my pocket and resumed digging.

I moved on and hooked up with Ronnie, the front-loader with NYC Transit. After two hours of not being used, we took it upon ourselves to start along Church Street clearing additional debris in front of the Post Office, the first building structurally sound across from the dangerously unstable World Trade tower 5.

Many of us chose not to wear our masks, donning them only when the smoke became unbearable. We did this not out of bravado, but for the sake of efficiency. Communication was impossible when wearing the masks, and they also collected humidity quickly to the point that water would literally dam up against your lips. In addition, to remove the mask to speak, you had to grab it with your gloved hands that were covered in dust and ash, at the risk of getting some in your eyes, which did not tickle, and generally required a trip to the nurses' station for an eyewash.

And, speaking of nurses—and the volunteers, and the Salvation Army, the Red Cross, and others—these people were true heroes. There were half a dozen structures at risk of falling, including the Millennium Hotel and I Liberty—both over fifty stories. If they had collapsed, they would easily have killed over a thousand people in and around the pile. These volunteers brought water, food, juice, socks, shirts, rain gear—you name it—to the workers on the site. They put themselves just as much at risk as the expert search-and-rescue teams. They are to be commended, and I was honored to be with them.

And it was dangerous. We were told that the foundations of many of the buildings had been severely compromised from the initial collapse. Lasers were trained on 5 World Trade Center, the Millennium Hotel, and I Liberty, and they were under constant surveillance by structural engineers and OSHA. Whenever there was too great a shift, the sirens went off. And this happened, again . . . and again . . . and again. Over five times on Thursday. The problem was that if the Millennium or Liberty went you needed to be ten to twenty blocks away when it happened, and none of us were cheetahs. So when the siren went, many ran, but most walked, not out of disrespect for the urgency of the potential collapse, but because we were tired, we wore heavy boots and gear, and we never would have made it. Several guys wrote their names and social security numbers on their arms in case of this happening—some wrote on both arms in case one limb were separated from the other.

I took a lunch break in an abandoned building with several ironworkers. Tough guys with tattoos. One talked about how this was our Pearl Harbor. I didn't openly argue with him, but I couldn't disagree more. Pearl Harbor was a military installation. Even the Pentagon was a military installation. This was our Nagasaki, our Sebrinka, our Guernica. But, I never saw despair or anger in anyone's face, and despite the scribblings of vengeance and revenge on the store windows and car windshields, I rarely heard a bitter word from these men and women. What I saw and witnessed was unbelievable determination, defiance toward danger, and the feeling that step by step, inch by inch, we would move forward from this.

In the late afternoon, Ronnie's crew was told to log out. Not that they wanted to, but they were union, and rules, especially union rules, were to be kept. Ronnie's boss, Fred Handy, told me they'd be back at 8 A.M. the next day and I could team up with them again if I wanted to.

With no immediate assignment, I turned to my trusty shovel and began working my way down the curb to the bottom of Vesey and the southeast end of the collapsed tower number seven. I was clearing eight to ten inches of soot-layered debris off the steps leading into the subway when several men passed by me to enter the subway. One turned back, as he didn't have a flashlight. I did, so I followed.

The tracks were flooded past the platform from the millions of gallons of water that had been poured into the subway and from hundreds of broken water mains. Kirin "Dutch" Smith, along with two other NYC Transit workers, two firefighters, and myself, made our way through a thirty-eight-inch-high subway airshaft and into the basement of Trade Center 2. The eerie silence was broken by the multiple beeps of computer alarms (I think). We made our way through corridors, were turned back twice by collapsed stairwells full of rubble, then suddenly, surprisingly, found ourselves staring up a partially destroyed escalator into the atrium of Trade Center 2. There was a reddish tint of the fading sun on the hazy, quiet interior. We were debating trying the escalator when, in the distance, the unmistakable wail of the warning sirens started up. "Get out! GET OUT!" were the words over Dutch's talkie, and we ran—I mean, ran—to get the hell out of there.

After resurfacing, Dutch reported the subway access to the search-and-recovery workers, and they took it from there. Unfortunately, as the story went all day, they found nothing. There was little news while we worked. With the disaster and debris covering several square miles, command was spotty at best. We found out four hours later that two firemen had been found alive. Sadly, I found out the next day, the story we had heard was merely repeated news from the day before: those two men had been pulled out the day before.

Dutch, a handsome Norwegian with piercing blue eyes that seemed to climb over his dust mask, allowed me to tag along with his crew, as we searched the subway for a phone junction networking box. We found it, locked, but with a very convincing screwdriver, we were able to pry open the door. As they entered, another worker and I looked for something to prop the door open. I spied a pay phone and pulled out my snips. I deftly sliced through the receiver wire and fumbled to jam the phone and line under the door. It held.

The subway platform was hot, but as we climbed a flight of stairs to the junction room, the heat spiked to between 105 and 110 degrees. We all trained our flashlights on the control box, as Dutch worked the phone connections, looking for live lines. We needed eight working connections. Many were dead. As the minutes ticked by, we became increasingly nervous about the temperature and the fact that we were directly underneath several very unsteady buildings and what remained of the towers. As we reached seven lines and hit a continuous row of dead lines, someone mentioned that we could use the phone on the platform if it was working (that, of course, was the line I had cut). The fellow—I never got his name—who had been with me made eye contact. Even with the masks, "Oops" was obvious in his expression. Fortunately, the gods smiled upon us, as Dutch snagged another clear line and one for backup, and we headed back to the surface. My screwup would stay with me and the fellow with the orange respirator. With the sketched phone lines and plans to distribute them the next day, we headed back to the office trailer. While resting I called home to Ariana. She had asked that I call her every two hours; I tried to adhere to that as best I could.

To be honest, she wasn't happy that I was there, particularly since I had come without telling her, in an effort to avoid an argument. Carter, my four-and-a-half-year-old, was next to her at home and asked to speak with me. Once on the phone, he excitedly asked me how it was going at the "construction site," and what type of machines I had ridden. I told him a big truck and a tractor and a bulldozer, too. From across the room, I saw Dutch catching my conversation and from my tone of voice and vocabulary he knew I was talking to my kid. His eyes softened and he suddenly looked very tired. As I hung up, he called to me, "Your boy, how old?" "Four and a half," I answered, "and a nineteen-month-old." "Five and three," he countered, the ages of his kids. We nodded silently, knowing that this was not the world that, two days ago, we hoped our children would live in.

Dutch and his crew were dismissed to pick up in the morning. I was again without a leader. Two Home Depot trucks drove by loaded with a couple thousand buckets. Someone yelled that they needed more on "the pile" for the bucket brigade. I followed the trucks. "The pile" was more like a pit, with jagged remnants of the two towers and three other buildings stabbing toward the sky. The task was simple. If you weren't a digger, you were a passer. You found an open space and waited for a bucket to reach you. If it was full, you passed it out. If it was empty, you passed it in. After a half hour or so of passing, a spot opened up on the pile, and I, like everyone else, dropped to my knees and began digging, at first, with my hands. But I soon uncovered a door handle, which worked remarkably well as a dagger and chisel. Much of my area was thick with cable and wires, and again my snips came in handy to cut through these. In my area, as soon as it was known that the tin snips were available, the diggers would call out "snips!" The snips would be tossed to them, they would use them, and then hold onto them until the next person called out for them. Much of our frustration came from digging for twenty or thirty minutes only to hit solid concrete—the plaza and courtyard area. Once you hit the plaza you had to move on, in search of a hole that kept going down.

Again, volunteers, defiant of the dangers, passed among us with water, Gatorade, food, and encouragement. Around 10 P.M., the wind began to pick up. Some glass and debris broke free of 2 World Financial Center and rained down on the western section of the pile, causing a mild panic. This was immediately followed by a loud pop of what most believe was a compressor hose, but the sound set into motion a massive, uncontrolled exodus from the western rim. As the rush reached a dangerous level, I sat down underneath a collapsed beam and found myself with two firemen. We all agreed we had no idea what was going on, but if any of the big buildings were coming down, there was no need to break a sweat, if we were about to die anyway. After ten uneasy minutes, we returned to digging. I didn't come across any remains that I know of. I was aware that all the buckets were to be sifted by forensic specialists off site. We were just to dig it up. After an hour or so, I took a break and stepped out. A policewoman quickly took my place.

I slowly made my way over to a mess area where rescuers were being fed. Three filthy and ragged firefighters sat hunched on buckets drinking bottled Evian water. As I approached, one offered his bucket and sat on the ground. I sat and they stared at me. One showed concern and offered me a clean wet towel to wash my face off. "To be honest, I have no idea what I look like," I said. "To be honest," replied one of the firemen, "absolute shit." We all laughed. It was a good laugh. "What's that in your hands?" asked another fireman. I glanced down to see the handle in my glove. "It's my shovel." "How's that working for you?" "I'm thinking of marketing them." Again, we laughed. They asked me where I was from. I asked them about bodies. "One," replied the towel lender. "He was like a jellyfish. He was completely there . . . just . . . soft." We didn't talk much after that. And I returned to the pile.

After another forty minutes, I realized it was time to get out—let the stronger, fresher volunteers in. I was tired and I wanted to lie down. I left my tin snips with a digger, and slowly made my way out of the pile. To my left and to my right, buckets of debris were handed past me and empty ones returned. No one was talking: everyone was concentrating on the job at hand. As I slowly made my way out of the site, I inquired about a place to rest. Did the Salvation Army or Red Cross have anything set up? No one knew. I knew that many were sleeping in the lobbies of the buildings still standing, but I wanted to be safe, at least for a little while. Turning up Church Street, I looked back to see hundreds running from the site. Another alarm had gone off. I was definitely not sleeping here tonight.

I used my cell phone and got half a dozen answering machines of friends in the Village area. I figured they had left town. I noticed a police car approaching me from behind and stuck out my thumb. The car stopped. The officer asked me where I was headed. I said, "St. Vincent's." He motioned for me to climb in. As we made our way up the street, he asked me if I was going to visit anyone there. I lied. I said a friend worked in that hospital. I was actually hoping I could find a place to sleep. The officer dropped me off at the emergency room entrance. As I got out, he called out to me. "Hey, thank you." "Sure," I replied and headed for the emergency room.

I had heard that they were using St. Vincent's for triage, and thought they might have beds set aside. The green-jacketed Caribbean gentleman who was part of hospital security politely told me there were no beds. As I turned to leave, he called to me.

"You look exhausted . . . maybe you should be admitted for exhaustion." As I tried to explain I didn't want to screw with paperwork, I noticed he had leaned back, opening the door with his shoulder, and was pointing at a set of benches. He smiled and without a word I walked past him to the bench and lay down. I was asleep within seconds. A gentle prodding woke me. I wasn't sure how long I was out—maybe ten minutes—but I opened my eyes to see half a dozen doctors and nurses in blue scrubs asking me if I was okay. I told them I was just beat and needed to rest. One nurse asked why I hadn't gone to the Salvation Army right around the block, where cots and hot food were available. Sheepishly, I admitted that no one had told me about it. As I stood, one nurse, name unknown, insisted on walking me around the corner and making sure I found a bed.

Entering the Salvation Army, I noted supplies stacked to the ceiling: food, water, socks, batteries, dog food, cookies, and hundreds of other things. My guide and I made our way through the path of stacked goods and upstairs to where thirty to forty cots were laid out. Very few were taken. Of the ones that were full, half of those were men completely passed out from exhaustion, in deep sleep. The others held men with pursed lips and blank looks staring straight at the ceiling. They paused to glance my way, then returned to their thousand-mile stares. Despite the fact that I had been up for over twenty hours, my nap at the hospital had left me wide awake. So I collected several of the free toiletries offered to us and went to the bathroom and shaved. My eyes were bloodshot, yet clear.

I think one of things I'll remember about this event was the eyes. It's how you communicated. With the masks and other various protective clothing and helmets, the only thing you could really focus on was the eyes. I remembered the saying that the eyes are windows to the soul. But they also can speak when the mind and voice cannot. During my time on the site, I had dozens of conversations with other workers in which not a word was uttered.

Eventually, I returned to my cot and lay back, joining others in staring at the ceiling. Hundreds of questions flashed through my head. Most of them began with "How?" or "Why?... Where? ... Who?... I drifted off to sleep. I awoke a little after six A.M. to find nearly every cot filled with an exhausted volunteer. I quickly dressed and grabbed several candy bars, Pop Tarts, a banana, and two Pepsis, and went downstairs to head out.

It had been raining all night, and it was pouring as I looked out. I thought of all that pulverized concrete remixing with water to become essentially new concrete and the weight it would add on the collapsed site. A Salvation Army volunteer provided me with a raincoat, which I put on, before heading out into the heavy drizzle.

I reached St. Vincent's, hoping to catch a ride down to the site. A police officer explained that if I wanted to help, I needed to go to the Jacob Javitz Center (some forty blocks away). I explained that I had already been down at the site and was intending to resume working with my NYC Transit crew. The officer apologized, and explained that owing to the president's visit, security was going to be tight. Disgusted, I walked away and headed south. I was going to work today. I stopped at a hardware store and bought two more pairs of tin snips, knowing they would be needed. The first police line turned me away, and I headed east on Fourteenth Street. A second police barricade also turned me away. When I reached the third police line on Church Street and demanded to see a superior officer, a captain (I think) approached me and I explained that I was with Dutch Smith's crew as a volunteer, and my I.D. was in the trailer four blocks away. All I needed was an escort to the trailer to verify this. The officer looked me up and down, then asked me for identification. "All I have is my driver's license," I said, exasperated. "Let me see it," he countered. I pulled out my driver's license and handed it to him. He looked at the license for a few seconds before handing it back. "OK, good luck." And he stepped aside. I thanked the officer and headed on down to the site, passing unchallenged several other police lines and soldiers.

The rain was cold. There was a hardness in each drop. Yes, it would keep down the dust, maybe the smoke, but it would also produce sludge. As I approached ground zero, I saw several rows of Port-a-Potties. I was happy. The day before, when we had to relieve ourselves, we did it indoors, in the lobbies and stairwells of the abandoned buildings. It was too dangerous to try to find bathrooms in the darkened buildings, and urinating on the streets seemed almost sacrilegious, considering it was one giant grave.

Unable to find my crew, I found a shovel and began making small piles of rubble, again working my way down Vesey Street. I again found myself at the subway entrance and resumed clearing the stairs. Since it was out of the rain, I was kicking up a fine amount of dust and put on my mask as I worked down the stairs. I paused to move a strip of metal, and when I stood up, I sensed something at the top of the stairs. I looked up. Through the dusty haze I saw a figure, all in black except for his clerical collar, which was white, as was his mask and hardhat. Our eyes met. Without a word, his eyes asked if I were OK. With my eyes I said I was fine. He moved on, and I resumed clearing.

They were limiting access to the pile because of the rain, and to be honest, it was fine with me. I knew they would have made a lot of progress in the night and that the chance of finding remains was far greater today. Call me a coward, but I didn't think it was something I could comfortably live with for the rest of my life, if I indeed found someone, or part of someone. The only signs of death I had come across had been on the street the day before. As I shoveled, I had come across two mourning doves—one without its head, another without wings, and I had found both discoveries very disquieting.

We had a few more siren warnings as the day progressed, and again, many of us chose not to run. The president came by, but the crew I had joined never saw him, even though he was just a block away. Considering that the blast site was over four square miles, a lot of things happened that many of us didn't know about. Friday saw a very heavy presence of soldiers near the site. Despite their military appearance in camouflage and gear, the awe and sheer disbelief was registered on many of these young faces. This was the soldiers' first taste of war . . . and it was in their own land.

I never tracked down Dutch's crew, but I did run into Mr. Handy and was able to hook up again with Ronnie.

Despite the rain, smoke continued to fill the blast zone. The smoke was like a fog: it would seem to almost evaporate, then suddenly engulf you and block out the light. And the smell. . . . Most people are familiar with campfires, even the smell of house fires, but the acrid smoke that haunted this site had a taste of its own. It's a taste I'll never forget. My last couple of hours were spent shoveling at the base of Vesey, as two front-loaders and a small bulldozer took bits of rubble out via a pedestrian bridge, blocking entrance to the Trade Center garage. I met Curtis Sliwa, the founder of the Guardian Angels, and gave him a brief rundown of the current status of the surrounding buildings. He looked pretty pissed. He had spent his life cleaning the streets of crime, and what lay before him was a crime against humanity.

Around 4:00 P.M., or so, Ronnie's crew had maxed their hours and were ordered to head out. I could have stayed, but I was tired. I knew if I left, I probably would not get back in . . . and . . . that was okay. It seemed like the right people were there now, and people like myself could just get in the way. I know many volunteers chose to stay on-site, sleeping in the abandoned buildings, so they could continue to work. God bless them. I missed my boys; I missed my wife. I had had enough of this place. I wanted to go back to my life. A stay-at-home dad may not sound romantic, but it sure looked good from here.

I took one last look at the jagged, angry remnants of the greatest buildings in the world, and turned to go. As I made my way uptown on Church Street, I passed several front-loaders waiting in line, ready to leave. Two men stepped out of their cabs and called to me. "David, you heading out?" Both these men, whom I had worked with the day before, remembered my name. I had no idea what theirs were. "Yes . . . I'm heading home." "God bless you—stay safe." I waved to them and stuck out my thumb at a passing police car one last time. The officer took me to Canal Street, to the barricades. I thanked her. She thanked me. And I walked down the stairs to the subway. A businessman stepped aside to let me pass. "Thank you for all you've done." I didn't feel like I had done that much, but I didn't know what else to say. "Sure," I replied, and continued down the stairs.

On the rush-hour train home to Manhasset that Friday, amidst the three-piece suits and button-down business folk, a lone, smoky-smelling former carpenter with a hard hat watched the world go by. Some stared and said nothing, but their eyes said, "Thank you." And a conductor slowly passed by, refusing to take my ticket.

December 11, 2001

I am now a fireman for my town of Manhasset, sworn in last week and supposed to pick up my "bunker gear" and dress blues from the main department today. Although my formal training lasts a year, I've reached the point that I can now fight fires among the same brave men I had the honor of working with at ground zero. The latest numbers note that rescue workers evacuated over twenty-six thousand people from the World Trade Center during and after the attack. Twenty-six thousand were home for the holidays.

In my garage is a small plastic case I've kept since working at ground zero. I retrieved from it the miniature painting of a three-masted ship that I brought back with me from the pile and that has been haunting me ever since. The tiny brush strokes were quite impressive, creating both waves breaking against the ship and the gentle clouds pushing it on its way. The tear from the shrapnel I had pulled out was minimal and I noticed again the name of the artist on the back of the painting, Sylvia L. Beckey. I wanted to find her. I needed to find her. I called the operator and, when a real person came on, I explained my situation. For several minutes we searched the directory listings in New York and Connecticut. I was about to call it quits when we found a Sylvia L. Beckey listed in Jersey City, a twelve-minute train ride from the Trade Center. There was one catch. The number was unlisted, and the operator could not give it to me. But she wanted to help, so she gave me her supervisor, who gave me the number of the Jersey City sheriff's department. Although sympathetic, they could not access a number without a court order. They referred me to the Liberty Island WTC missing persons office, which in turn led me to victim's assistance at Pier 94 in Manhattan. Tony, who worked the phone there, could not access a number. "Just tell me this," I asked, "is she listed as dead or missing?" No, she was not. At least, though whoever had the painting may be gone, perhaps Sylvia would know who that was and the owner or a relative might want it back. Tony checked his computer files for additional clues. "I have here on the office records that there was a Sylvia L. Beckey as a vice-president of a commercial firm . . . in tower one." Bingo.

Tony gave me the website address for Sylvia's company, but phone, fax, and e-mail lines did not work. Even three months after the disaster, the phone system in lower Manhattan is still primitive at best. On the site, I found a link to the firm's legal representation, and discovered from the lawyers' bios that one had gone to Catholic University, as I had. When I reached her, I gave my spiel: her firm represented Sylvia's company. Would a senior partner know how to contact her? She said she'd call back within the hour, and when she did, she had Sylvia's address. The senior partner said Sylvia had recently relocated to Houston, Texas, and that she'd taken up painting in the last few years and was devastated at the loss of all the paintings that hung on her office wall. He thanked me for contacting them as Sylvia would be very happy to have one painting back. I was thankful to send this painting on. An object that came into my possession held life.

On September 11, I went to the center of a great wound in our world and somehow I was able to find humor and art and examples of humanity and compassion. Three months to the day after that day when our hearts briefly stopped, I mailed the carefully wrapped painting to Sylvia L. Beckey. And, as I left the post office, I cried, but they were tears of hope.

A CANDLELIGHT VIGIL AT THE FIREMAN'S MONUMENT

BY RUSSELL FREEDMAN

I have always known
That, at last, I would take this road,
But I did not know it would be today.
— Narihira, ninth-century Japanese poet

The street I live on in New York City, a quiet stretch of West 100th, is known fondly to my neighbors as "A Monumental Block." It's an old-fashioned block tucked away between West End Avenue and Riverside Drive, a haphazard mix of brownstones and apartment houses built in the early decades of the last century, shaded in summer by Japanese elms planted by our block association, and anchored at its western end, where the street dips steeply downhill toward the Hudson River, by the limestone and marble Fireman's Monument.

Dedicated in 1912, the monument rises grandly from a windy terrace overlooking Riverside Park. A large bronze tablet on the front of the monument depicts three frenzied horses pulling a fire engine, racing to the rescue as shirt-sleeved firemen urge them on. Beneath the tablet, water flows from a stone lion's mouth into an oval pool that sometimes attracts neighborhood dogs, who plunge in and splash around.

The rear wall of the monument, facing 100th Street, has this inscription:

TO THE MEN OF THE FIRE DEPARTMENT

OF THE CITY OF NEW YORK

WHO DIED AT THE CALL OF DUTY

SOLDIERS IN A WAR THAT NEVER ENDS

THIS MEMORIAL IS DEDICATED

BY THE PEOPLE OF A GRATEFUL CITY

Every autumn, on the second Wednesday of October, the monument becomes the site of a memorial service held to honor those heroic dead. Fire Department brass and men and women from the ranks assemble in their crisp dress uniforms for a brief, moving ceremony that always ends with the same tribute—the mournful strains of "Amazing Grace," played by bagpipers from the department's pipe and drum corps.

In the year 2001, for the first time in memory, that traditional service did not take place in October. Because so many firefighters had lost their lives in the World Trade Center disaster, a special memorial service was scheduled for later in the year. In the meantime, the Fireman's Monument on 100th Street became the site of a candlelight vigil that arose spontaneously following the September 11 terrorist attack.

At 8:46 on that innocently bright and sunny morning, American Airlines flight 11, piloted by terrorists, slammed into the north tower of the Trade Center and burst into a fireball. Eighteen minutes later, a second hijacked jet, United Airlines flight 175, hit the south tower, spewing a fiery cloud of debris into the air.

Firefighters raced to the scene, along with police officers, medical personnel, and other rescue workers. They arrived to find thousands of horrified office workers fleeing for their lives, running away from the burning buildings. The firefighters ran inside. As any child can tell you, that is simply what firemen do. They rushed into the twin towers and began to climb the stairs, searching for survivors, and when they found them, guiding them back down the stairs to safety.

People who managed to escape down the staircases of the doomed buildings reported afterward that the most remarkable sight during their descent was the wave of determined firemen carrying heavy equipment and climbing up those stairs, advancing toward the burning sky. "They were perspiring profusely, exhausted," said David Frank, who escaped from the seventy-eighth floor of 1 World Trade Center, the first tower hit. "And they had to go all the way up to the nineties—straight into hell."

Louis G. Lesce was on his way down from the eighty-sixth floor. "One fireman stopped to take a breath, and we looked each other in the eye," he reported. "He was going to a place where I was damn well trying to get out of. I looked at him, thinking, 'What are you doing this for?' He looked at me as if he knew very well. 'This is my job.'"

As the rescuers pressed upward, the two blazing sky-scrapers, weakened by fires raging on their upper floors, suddenly and shockingly collapsed, one after the other. A quarter-mile high, the elevators would take you up 110 stories in fifty-eight seconds. Now, the buildings crumbled in less than a minute. They dropped from the skyline. The top floors buckled out, spraying tiny glass and metal shards, and each building sank down into itself, leaving a smoldering mountain of twisted steel and shattered glass, dust, and debris. Firemen who were inside the buildings trying to rescue people, and many of those who were outside at ground level trying to contain the fires, were buried beneath the great heap of rubble. The stunned firefighters who had survived regrouped in the ruins. Then, they went back to work.

In all, 343 firemen lost their lives that day—the worst single loss by far that the department had ever suffered. Until then, the biggest loss of life for the Fire Department was in 1966, when twelve men were killed in a fire on East 23rd Street.

This time, entire companies were lost. Among the dead was a Fire Department chaplain, Father Mychal Judge, crushed by falling debris while administering to the injured. Two brothers, Peter Langone, a firefighter, and Thomas Langone, a New York City police officer, both lost their lives in the disaster. A father and son, Joseph Angelini and Joseph Angelini, Jr., were killed. So were several top-ranking commanders and chiefs, and many rookies, some of whom were fighting their first big fire. The elite units suffered most. The department's Special Operations Command, trained to handle the worst disasters, lost 95 of its 452 men, including its chief, Raymond Downey.

On the day of the attack, the people of New York began to leave bouquets of flowers and messages of condolence and gratitude at firehouses all over the city, at parks and public squares, and at the Fireman's Monument on 100th Street. The monument became a colorful outdoor shrine, awash in flowers and small American flags and memorial candles that somehow were kept burning day and night. Among the offerings was a giant wreath of chrysanthemums and gladioli sent by the Hertfordshire Fire and Rescue Service in Hertford, England, accompanied by a card that said, "We are thinking of those courageous firefighters who lost their lives in the line of duty. They will always be remembered."

Taped to the sides of the monument and along the rim of the pool and on the walls circling the terrace were scores of letters, poems, notes, and drawings from children: "Thank you for protecting us—Emma, age 4"; "In memory of the brave men who died in the terrorist attack—Kevin, 10"; "To those of you who lost your lives and the families you leave behind, we wish you peace. You will be missed. You are heroes—Sincerely, Sarah and Ana." A small collage of pressed flowers held a card that said, simply, "Thank you—Alina, 3 years." And a card with the Chinese character for "love" had been left by a young immigrant named Xiaoming.

Now leaflets began to appear in the neighborhood, posted on doorways and in apartment lobbies and elevators, announcing a candlelight vigil to be held at the monument at 8 P.M. on Friday, September 14—three days after the terrorist attack. When I arrived with some friends, shortly before 8 that evening, several hundred people had already gathered. The crowd surrounded the monument on all sides, packed the terrace in front, and spilled down the stone steps leading to Riverside Park. Everyone, it seemed, was holding burning candles—stubby white prayer candles, long tapered dinner-table candles, fat memorial candles encased in many-colored glass cylinders.

People spoke in whispers or low murmurs, if they spoke at all, awed into silence by the thought of bravery on such a scale. I saw many of my neighbors as I looked around, friends I had known for years, and many unfamiliar faces, as well. Parents cradled infants in their arms and held youngsters by the hand. Couples and friends stood close with arms around each other. People hugged as they arrived and met. Some folks wept. On this warm September evening, a gentle breeze washed across the terrace. Hundreds of candles flickered and glowed.

I wondered if anyone in the crowd had lost a loved one in the attack. And I was aware, as were so many others, I am sure, that the everyday life we take for granted—with its comfortable routines, its safety, its security, its freedom—is a momentary gift that can be snatched away. Those 343 firemen, along with 3,000 workers at the World Trade Center, victims of eighty nationalities, men and women they were trying to save, would never go home. And yet, for those at the monument that evening, the catastrophe had created a powerful sense of community, had drawn neighbors and strangers together in a communal expression of grief and gratitude and mutual support. At that moment, we needed each other. We knew that the firemen who had given their lives to rescue others had died to save strangers, so it did not seem strange for us to be there.

Someone began to sing "We Shall Overcome," and from the edges of the crowd other voices joined in, and the chorus swelled. Then, we sang "God Bless America." Afterward, as if guided by some unseen hand, the entire crowd began to move slowly up 100th Street, shielding burning candles with cupped hands, heading for the local firehouse three-and-a-half blocks away. We made our way across West End Avenue, across Broadway, across Amsterdam Avenue, while at each intersection, cars stopped and waited for the procession to pass.

The firehouse on 100th Street stands in the middle of the block, next to the police station. The crowd collected out in front, filling the street, extending up and down the block in both directions, as firefighters gathered in the doorway.

"Thank you!" someone shouted. Then others took up the cry, calling out, "Thank you!" "God bless you!" "You're all our heroes!" And, again, people began to sing, forcefully and with feeling, belting out the words of "God Bless America," singing for all those souls who had been lost, singing for ourselves, to soothe our sorrowful hearts and help us stand, and singing for our audience of shirt-sleeved firemen, standing impassively in the doorway of their firehouse, accepting the gratitude of the crowd with silent grace, knowing, as we knew, that their feat of courage can never be repaid.

CHILDREN OF WAR

BY JOAN BAUER

"What are you afraid of?" Hanrahan asks me.

That's easy.

"I'm afraid of getting on an airplane. I'm afraid of getting blown up in the subway. I'm afraid of going across the Brooklyn Bridge because it might get dynamited. I'm afraid I'll be in a building and a plane will crash through it. I'm afraid my family will die. I'm afraid a bomb will go off in a store, some nuclear weapon will be detonated in my bathroom. I'm afraid of anthrax. I'm afraid I'll be somewhere and a terrorist will show up with explosives in his nostrils and . . ."

"Nostril bombs, Liza?"

"Some guy had bombs in his sneakers, Hanrahan. Those guys will use anything to get past security."

"What else?"

"I'm afraid I won't ever feel normal."

"You're not normal."

"This isn't useful, Hanrahan."

"Well, it is really. I read this article about fear and it said the worst part of fear is the stuff we don't admit."

"Aren't you afraid of anything?"

"Yes." Hanrahan looks from the rail at the Brooklyn Heights Promenade across the East River to where the Trade Center used to be. "I'm scared that it was so easy for these men to bring down the towers. I'm scared we weren't better protected. I'm scared we took things for granted."

"Me, too."

"But, it's safer now, Liza, than before."

"How can you say that?"

"Because we know more now. And when you know more, you can do more to protect yourself."

"I think, Hanrahan, those guys have a lot of surprises left."

"They're not that smart."

I sigh. Hanrahan can be so thick.

I'm not sure why I keep walking to the Promenade.

Familiarity, maybe.

Maybe I walk there expecting to wake up from the bad dream.

I walk there before school in the mornings. I walk there late in the day.

I tell myself, if I look at the big empty place in the Manhattan skyline where the World Trade Center used to be, if I look at it long enough, maybe I won't be afraid.

This doesn't seem to be working.

I was at school when it happened.

The lights went out at 8:48 that morning.

I'll tell you what I remember most.

The smoke.

How it came and hovered over the city. How it got in our eyes and in our mouths and on our teeth until the smell of it took over.

I would go inside and try to close the windows to keep it out, but it wouldn't stay out. It was like fear that knows how to creep through the cracks, slip under doors, and make its presence known.

There were stories here in Brooklyn of how shoes landed in the street and papers flew from the explosion across the river. There were ashes in people's backyards. Then, that night, the candles began burning in so many windows. The photos of the missing went up at bus stops and stores. So many in our neighborhood. The stories in the news of the people who had been saved, the firemen from Red Hook who were all killed. The man on the 92nd floor who wanted a Krispy Kreme donut and took the elevator all the way down to the street of the World Trade tower and missed getting killed because of a donut.

I couldn't go to school.

I sat and watched the news. Watched everything there was to say about it on TV. Couldn't move from the couch.

I think I was waiting for someone to tell me why it really happened.

But no one did.

No one could.

All the broadcasters were trying to explain about Islam and the Middle East and the Taliban and Osama bin Laden and the differences between fundamentalist hatred and regular old hatred.

I heard about the hijackers who had flown the planes into the towers killing themselves and all those people. The hijackers who thought that act would get them into a special place in heaven.

I watched Mayor Giuliani being so brave and telling people that New Yorkers were going to rebuild. I watched President Bush explain about terrorists and how we couldn't let them continue this way.

I saw the flags go up everywhere.

By the end of the week, my dad knew eight people who had died.

I knew four.

What I want to know is why.

Not what the TV people say.

Not what the reporters tell me.

I want to know how anybody could do that.

You can see it all on the news, but when you stand on the Promenade in Brooklyn Heights, when you hear the roar of the Brooklyn Queens Expressway under your feet, when you look up at the Manhattan skyline and realize that the towers are really, really gone—then you know how much they took.

On September 11, I was going to meet with Mr. Shapiro, my college counselor, and give him my almost finished essay for my college applications. I'd worked on it so hard, bled over every adjective, and now it seemed small and unimportant.

I'd changed. I didn't know how.

But I had.

In school they told us about posttraumatic stress disorder.

We all had it.

We couldn't eat, couldn't sleep, couldn't concentrate.

"You have to write it," Hanrahan said. "You have to finish your essay; get into college."

"I'll finish it," I kept saying.

Some telemarketer actually called my mom on September 12 and asked if she wanted a credit card from some bank in the Midwest. She screamed at the guy, hung up.

Funny how the world can go on when you're at war.

"You've got to write it," Hanrahan says to me.

It's October.

"I can't." I sit down on the park bench on the Promenade.

"Just write how you feel, Liza. You've got to get it out."

"I can't think about college. Everything has changed."

"They don't want you to go to college!" I look up. "What do you mean?"

"The terrorists. They don't think women should go to college. You're just letting them rule your life."

"I am not."

"Yes, you are. You're buying into their game to make you afraid and keep you afraid."

"I don't want to talk about this."

"That's why they're called terrorists."

"They blew up buildings, Hanrahan. They know how to kill people! Their big plan has nothing to do with my college essay!"

"Sure it does. They just want you afraid so you can't function. If you can't function, you can't learn. If you can't learn, you won't be a big threat in the world."

"I was never going to be a big threat."

"Yes, you were. You were going to be a teacher."

"I know what you're doing, Hanrahan!"

"What am I doing?"

"You're trying to get me mad, aren't you?"

He smiled. "Your face is red and you're screaming."

"You're impossible!"

"Don't you want to be a teacher?"

I shrug.

"Is there a better time to be a teacher than now?"

"I just don't . . ."

"What?"

"I don't know what the world's going to be like."

"Did you know on September 10?"

"That's an unfair question, Hanrahan."

"Why? Did you know what the world was going to be like? Did you have it all mapped out?"

"You know what I mean."

"We didn't know then and we don't know now."

"It's more complicated. It's harder now."

"Yes."

"I wrote an essay about going whitewater rafting, Hanrahan. All that happened was that I fell out of the boat. I thought it was some big life-changing moment."

"So change it."

I'm at my computer trying to figure out why I want to be a teacher anyway.

I don't know how to fight in this war.

I'm not a soldier.

I'm not a rescue worker.

I close my eyes and can see the people jumping from the buildings.

I hear a siren and wonder if it's happened again.

I didn't expect to know war in my lifetime. I never once thought about it.

I think about the people who gave themselves to the fight. The firemen, the rescue workers, the men who knew they were going to die on that hijacked airplane bound for Washington, D.C. They rushed the cockpit, caused the plane to crash in a Pennsylvania field.

They went down fighting.

I don't think any story touched me more than that.

We've got more power than we think.

That's why I want to teach.

Thanksgiving came and went.

Christmas tried to come. No one much feels like Christmas.

I go into stores, but don't buy presents. I just back out, shaking my head at all the stuff I don't want.

My mom asks me what I want for Christmas. I don't know.

A tree goes up by the Promenade with an American flag flying from its top.

I keep thinking of all the people who lost someone. I keep thinking about how easily life can change.

Hanrahan drags me down to the Promenade. It isn't all that cold. We've had such mild weather.

He puts a pad and paper in my hand.

"Write it," he says. "Write your essay. I dare you."

And I do.

We are left with the images that we will never forget.

They've been branded on our minds. They are part of us now.

Part of our past. Part of our future.

Gradually, the pictures will fade, the shadows will take over. We'll tell ourselves we should be over it now.

But we're not over it.

Not yet.

Maybe not ever.

I stand at the Promenade in Brooklyn Heights and look across the East River to where the Trade Center had been. I've walked here all my life, walked here with my dog, walked here with my friends. I've Rollerbladed and eaten pizza here, I've laughed, been kissed (once well, once badly), but I never cried on the Promenade until September 11.

I stand next to the piles of flowers, the photos of the missing, the candles flickering, the flags flying, the people standing quietly in clusters, holding coffee cups, holding each other, remembering the smell of smoke and death that settled over my city.

We are the children of war.

They took our parents, our sisters, our brothers, and our neighbors.

They turned planes into bombs.

A perfect sunny day became a horror.

We keep talking about where we were when it happened.

We'll always talk about it in some way.

"Where were you?"

I was in school.

The lights went out at 8:48 when the first plane hit.

No one knew what had happened.

Then gradually the news came.

We'll tell our children about it and our grandchildren.

Mostly, we'll turn it over and over in our minds, trying to make sense of what can never be understood.

If there are solutions, I want to help find them.

I think one of the ways to find them is through teaching. I don't know what really qualifies anyone to stand in front of a classroom and teach, other than wanting to make things better, wanting to share ideas, wanting to be part of a community of learners.

I am a New Yorker. I smelled the smoke, saw the ash from the towers, felt the fear settle over my shoulders, had the nightmares, lit the candles, went to the funerals. I wish to God that none of it had ever happened and I thank God that I was here when it did. I've been changed forever—that much I know. And because of that, I want to teach. I want to teach because I want to learn and understand. I believe we have a choice in this world, we, the children of war. We can learn from the hate, we can learn how to stop it, or we can learn to hate even more.

I mail the essay with three college applications the next day, a week before Christmas.

"OK," Hanrahan says. "Now we wait."

"I'm not good at that."

"I know."

"It doesn't seem like Christmas."

"I know."

"Everything's changed."

"Not everything," he says and points to the Brooklyn Bridge, the Empire State Building, the Staten Island Ferry crossing the harbor, and the Statue of Liberty still holding her torch for all the world to see.

VOICES

BY SONYA SONES

> I am the one
> who'd just fallen
> in love.
>
> I am the one
> who was pregnant
> with twins.
>
> I am the one
> who'd traveled from Kansas
> to see the view from the top.
>
> We are just some
> of thousands more,
> of thousands and thousands more.

I am the one
who'd just
gotten engaged.

I am the one
whose birthday
it was.

I am the one
who'd donated blood
only the day before.

We are just some
of thousands more,
of thousands and thousands more.

I am the one
who had such a bad cold
that I almost called in sick.

I am the one
who fought with my wife
before I came to work.

I am the one
who'd just found out
my cancer was in remission.

We are just some
of thousands more,
of thousands and thousands more.

I am the one
who would have met
the man of my dreams tomorrow.

I am the one
who would have been
bar mitzvahed on Saturday night.

I am the one
who would have discovered
a simple cure for AIDS.

We are just some
of thousands more,
of thousands and thousands more.

I am the one
who looked up from my desk
and first saw the plane bearing down.

I am the one
whose heart gave out
just before it struck.

I am the one
who thought of my dog
waiting for me to come home.

I am the one
who held my daughter close to me
and prayed.

I am the one
who phoned my son
and didn't know what to say.

I am the one
who reached out in the dark
to find a hand to hold.

We are just some
of thousands more,
of thousands and thousands more.

We are the ones
who were blown
through the glass.

We are the ones
who were
buried alive.

We are the ones
who did not die fast,
the ones who felt the fire.

We are just some
of thousands more,
of thousands and thousands more.

We are the ones
who rushed in
to help.

We are the ones
who were on
those planes.

We are the ones
who can't
rest in peace.

Dead
or
alive.

We are
the ones
who loved them.

We are
the ones
they loved.

We are just some
of millions more,
of millions and millions more.

SEARCHING FOR HISTORY

Putting 9/11 in the Context of a Personal Past

SEARCHING FOR HISTORY

In trying to make sense of the events of 9/11, each of the authors in this section has looked for context in his or her own personal past. Jim Murphy, for example, remembers when, as a young man, he visited the site of the World Trade Center, then still under construction. Jim Giblin recalls the emotions and concerns he felt as a boy during Pearl Harbor and later as a young New York editor during the Cuban missile crisis. Avi, too, recalls his boyhood and the horror he felt when he thought he'd killed a bird with his precious new BB rifle. For Kyoko Mori, watching birds at the feeder outside her window evokes memories of the stories she heard as a girl in Japan of the destruction that rained from the sky during the Second World War. Susan Cooper, too, recalls World War II and the sense of community she felt as a girl growing up in England, a country then under attack.

EIGHTY STORIES UP WITH
UNCLE BUDDY

BY JIM MURPHY

The phone rang that Sunday morning in 1970, well before the sun had come up. I was a little sleepy when I answered the phone, but I still recognized my uncle Buddy's voice on the other end of the line saying, "Jimmy, there's a problem at one of our buildings in the City. Get dressed, and I'll be right over to get you."

I began to ask a few questions—what building?—what sort of problem?—what about breakfast? But Uncle Buddy cut me short by telling me he had to make a couple of other calls, and then hung up.

While I got into my work clothes, I processed his message. The City, I knew, was New York City. Uncle Buddy was the foreman for a large construction company helping to put up a number of buildings there. Since I was working as a tin knocker on the Grace Building on 42nd Street near the New York Public Library, I assumed that was the building in question.

But what could have happened to require a predawn trip? I both dislike and love mysteries, so while I put on my heavy checked shirt, pants, and wool socks—it was a bitter-cold November day made worse by a nasty, gusting wind—I tried to puzzle it out. Had we left supplies or equipment someplace on the site that needed moving? Did we have to finish up a section quickly so another phase of work could begin? Both situations had occurred recently, but neither would need fixing on a Sunday. And neither would have prompted the "this is a real emergency" tone in my uncle's voice. I tied the laces of my scuffed and battered work boots and picked up my yellow hard hat, just as Uncle Buddy's car horn sounded out front of the house.

The mystery was explained as my uncle sped off into the dark to pick up two other men. He hadn't mentioned which building it was because he didn't want me to tell my mother where I'd be. I was twenty-three years old then and staying temporarily with my parents, and Uncle Buddy knew perfectly well that my mother would be up with the sound of the phone and asking questions, which was true. She disliked and loved mysteries, too. But because I knew nothing, I could tell her with an honest face that I didn't know.

My uncle had gotten me the job as a favor to my mother, though my mother had made him promise that I would never, ever be up too high or in dangerous places. This rule we broke immediately (without telling her, of course) because, as Uncle Buddy explained, "If you get the money, you do the work." For my part, I loved being up thirty and forty stories and looking out over Manhattan rooftops with their wooden water tanks, hidden garden patios, and blinking neon signs.

What's the big deal this time? I wanted to know. "We're going to the twin towers," he replied.

The World Trade Center was the big nut in terms of construction back in 1970, with two side-by-side 110-story office towers the crowning centerpiece. They would rise to become the tallest structures in New York City, and one of them (because of its television antennae) would reign briefly as tallest in the world. I'd asked if I could work on them several months before, and my uncle's answer was a lovingly gruff, "Are you crazy? Your mother would kill me."

When he explained what needed fixing that morning, I understood the strained tone of his voice. An hour or so before, pieces of decking had begun falling off the seventy-ninth or eightieth floor of one of the not yet completed towers. This was a lot more complicated than it might appear at first, so some explanation is needed here.

Ironworkers put up the metal skeleton of a building, with us tin knockers trailing them by two or three stories. Our job was to position long, corrugated sheets of metal—the decking—on the bare steel beams and weld them in place. These sheets were usually three feet wide and from fifteen to twenty feet long, and were so heavy that four workers were needed to move each one.

After the sheets were secured, cuts were made for stairwells, elevators, water and steam pipes, air-conditioning ducts, and anything else that needed to go through the floors. The carpenters would follow us, putting up wooden forms or borders around the outside of the building and all of the openings on the floor. Reinforcing rods were laid across the decking by ironworkers, and then came another group of laborers driving motorized wheelbarrows to pour cement over the entire area. The smoothed and dried cement was the basis of the building's floors.

Of course, many more people were needed to get a building, especially a very tall building, up—elevator and crane operators, plumbers and electricians, Sheetrockers, plasterers, glaziers, and tilers, to name a few. Then you had the truck drivers bringing in all of the construction materials; the suppliers, who made those materials; plus the architects, electrical and structural engineers, who drew up the plans and made out the lists of what would be needed. And don't forget the city inspectors, who checked that the work was being done correctly, or the police, who insured that deliveries could be made as easily as possible. One book on building skyscrapers lists over sixty separate skilled trades and professions needed to put such a structure up. A building site, I came to realize, was like a giant, vertical ant colony with thousands of people scurrying here and there, top to bottom, doing their special kind of work.

The most obvious problem with decking flying off a building was its potential to injure or kill someone below, or to damage streets, cars, and sidewalks. Luckily, this was happening in the middle of the night, so few people were about just then. That section of town wasn't heavily populated at the time either, so not many cars were on the surrounding streets, as I recall. The next problem was that the decking itself would be damaged and unusable and because all of the ordering of materials was done weeks and months in advance, this might potentially hold up work (ours and many of those below us) for days or even weeks. Finally, the falling sheets might damage sections of our building or the tower next to it, which was just beginning construction, if memory serves me, and this would cause additional delays. A disaster of sizable proportions might very well be in the making as we hurried through the Holland Tunnel into New York.

When we arrived at the lower Manhattan site, the police had already blocked off the streets and sidewalks to traffic and pedestrians. No one had been injured, according to the first policeman my uncle spoke to, and we could see three pieces of decking on Liberty Street, all within two hundred feet of each other. Things looked fairly contained, and my uncle breathed a sigh of relief—until another policeman told him that at least three other pieces had drifted farther west, one landing in West Street and the other two nearly reaching the Hudson River. Plus two other pieces had crashed down somewhere between the two construction sites.

My uncle's upset and concern grew when the second policeman told him one sheet had barely missed hitting him and his police cruiser. He'd pulled up, he told us, gotten out of his car, and glanced skyward. Far above, he could see what he described as "this thing" floating in the air, turning around lazily, like a giant, rippled potato chip, and then, suddenly, it seemed to gain speed and came slamming down with a deafening, metallic roar.

The policeman hadn't waited around to examine the crumpled metal or even to think about how close a call he'd just had. He'd jumped back into his car and retreated to a safer position, though with a gusting wind, who knew how far the decking might fly? I was amazed at the matter-of-fact way he'd ended his story, with, "D--- thing could've cut me in half."

By this time, my uncle was not only concerned, but angry. He wasn't the foreman on this job. A man who lived in central New Jersey was, but since that foreman wouldn't have been able to round up help and get to the site for several hours, the job and all of the responsibility had fallen to my uncle. Uncle Buddy spent a few moments detailing in extremely colorful language what he thought about the other foreman and his crew for being so sloppy and irresponsible. Clearly, they hadn't secured an open pile of decking correctly to withstand the wind.

While he vented, I looked up at the building, or better, at the steel columns, trusses, girders, and beams that soared up toward the still dark sky. Massive. Monumental. Imposing. And scary, too! I would read later that each side of the building was 400 feet long and, when completed, the towers would be 1,350 feet tall. That cold morning, all I knew was that it was very BIG and I felt very, very small in comparison.

Then it was to work. First, the other two men were told to get the crumpled pieces of metal off the streets and to a place where no one would trip over them. The wind had settled down some by this time, and the police said it had been over a half hour since anything new had come down, so maybe the situation had stabilized. Still, my uncle sent them off with a grumbled warning: "Don't go and get hit by one of these things."

Next, he and I went to find the decking before more was blown off the building. Fortunately, the security guards had been alerted that we would be there, and the chain-link gates had been unlocked and opened. My uncle spent several minutes talking with one of the guards, trying to find out exactly how many pieces of decking had fallen. The guard shrugged. Six, maybe seven. He didn't really know. A number could have sailed off unnoticed and landed out of his hearing. Next, he pointed us in the right direction and described where the staircase was, and we scurried as fast as we could to get inside the structure.

I did not have much time to study the interior. Where we entered some walls had already been put up, and there were building materials and pieces of equipment stored where we went through. Although the sun was beginning to peek over the horizon, and some lights were on inside, the place was still pretty dim.

Up the stairs we went, Uncle Buddy grumbling loudly every step of the way. He'd been told an elevator operator would be on hand to give us a lift, but clearly he was taking his time getting to the site. They always seemed to do that! Around the fifth floor, he also began wondering why the other two guys hadn't joined us yet, and assumed they'd gotten lost somewhere or stopped for a smoke. I suggested they'd gone looking for a place to have breakfast, mostly just to get a rise out of my uncle. Which it did.

After taking these first flights rather quickly, my uncle slowed us to a modestly fast pace, joking that he didn't want to have a heart attack before reaching the top. My uncle loved to talk and always seemed to have a knot of people around him, whether at family gatherings or on a job, listening to his stories and laughing at his jokes. So I knew our trip up would not be a silent journey.

Generally, he was a good-natured, cheerful man, kidding anyone near, trying to keep things from getting too serious. He was a big, burly man who enjoyed a good time. But he could be gruff when necessary, and I'd heard him bark out orders to keep a job moving forward, too. He'd enlisted in World War II when he was sixteen (with his parents' permission), and had become a sergeant and been in four major battles before he was nineteen, so I had an idea where his ability to command attention and lead had developed.

Still, there was something more to him than a simple desire to be listened to or get a job done. He really cared about family, friends, and acquaintances, and wanted to help them if at all possible (though he'd never say so out loud). That's why he always made sure his friends had work, why he went out of his way to get a job for a nephew who was waiting for one in publishing to open up, why everybody called on him when something needed to be done. Of course, he grumbled about the imposition and burden, about the way his phone never stopped ringing. But secretly he was proud that everyone turned to him, and that he could usually answer their requests.

The first ten flights went fairly fast, but it seemed to take a lot longer to cover the next ten. So by the time we had reached a floor with a crudely painted number 40 on the girder nearest the stairs, the sky had brightened considerably.

Less finishing work had been done up here—the cement floor was in place, some pipes and ducting were poking up in places, and great, flapping walls of canvas tarp stretched all over where crews were spraying fireproofing material on the steel. Still, the space seemed more open and expansive than those below.

My uncle told me to wait near the stairs, in case the other two appeared, and then he went off to ring the elevator buzzer. Maybe the operator had arrived and we could ride the rest of the way. No such luck; in fact, the elevator wouldn't run until nine o'clock or so.

At the fiftieth or fifty-fifth floor, we halted because we heard sounds below us, which turned out to be the other two men, who soon caught up with us. Not many floors later, we entered territory where only a modest amount of work had been done—the floors poured, some wood railings built around the elevator cuts, a few light bulbs hung on wire—a wide expanse of space, all of it swept by a steady wind.

The wind is the constant up there. When it is a calm day at ground level, it is always windy above twenty stories. On a breezy day below, the wind at that height can feel ferocious. I remember having my work gloves on and my hands jammed in my coat pocket, my head down to keep the cold out of my face and my eyes, which had begun to tear.

The steps ended, which meant we were nearly there. We were on a floor of corrugated metal; directly above us was a floor covered with inch-thick wood planks (a safety requirement of the city so that if an ironworker above falls, he'll only fall two stories—I loved that it was always referred to as "only" two stories!). The decking that was falling came either from the wood floor above or from the open steel above that.

We located the ladder we would need to climb to the next floor, stored under several hundred pounds of building material so it wouldn't blow off like our decking. My uncle said the foreman for our company should have taken some lessons from the carpenters on how to secure things. Just before we climbed the ladder, my uncle said very sternly, "I don't want anybody hurt up here, understand? So don't go and do anything stupid. And don't let your hats blow over either. That's all I need just now." We all mumbled, "Yes" and "Sure" and "No kidding." Then, in a slightly quieter voice he added, "You especially, Jimmy." He didn't have to add, "or your mother will kill me."

I wish I could provide a wildly dramatic ending to this, one with some high steel heroics and a near miss or two. But the truth, I'm happy to say, is a lot more low-key. The tin knockers on the tower had been putting decking on the open steel above the wood floor, opening one pile of decking at a time. When quitting time came, they still had half a pile left and, as suspected, had hastily tossed heavy wire cable and pieces of wood on top to hold it in place. During the night, the strong wind and maybe the movement of the building had shaken the wire and wood off, followed by the decking.

The piles had been set in from the edge, but when the wind flipped up a piece, the wide metal caught the wind like a sail and away it went, first to crash to the wood floor and then to fly off the building. Nine had gone over; one was still on the wood floor; another ten or so pieces remained on the pile, the top piece vibrating and waiting for the next big gust to come along.

First, one man went up a ladder and stood holding down one end of the decking against the wind. I had the other side. My uncle and the other man went off to round up materials to tie and hold down the decking.

I remember thinking that my job was about as daring and dangerous as holding an elevator door open. Less, really. After holding the pile down with my hands for a minute or so, I finally sat on it, leaning back and glancing around at the field of beams and columns surrounding me.

When my uncle spotted me a few minutes later, he said, "Putting that college education of yours to good use, I see." It was his first real quip of the morning, an indication that his sense of tension was easing. He continued ribbing me about my work ethic, while he and the other man tied the pile in several places with a heavy rope and weighted it down with cinder blocks. The one piece on the wood floor was brought away from the edge of the building and also weighted down.

After these loose sheets were secured, we checked all of the other piles of unopened decking to be sure the metal bands strapped around each load were still fastened tightly. Finally, we examined the floors below to see if a stray piece had blown onto another, lower floor or caused any sort of damage. Things that fall off a tall building tend to be sucked into it, but in this case, we assumed the wind had kept them away.

Yes, I did get to stand at the edge of an open side, one arm locked securely around a gigantic girder, with the other hand holding my hard hat in place as I leaned out a little to look down. The Statue of Liberty was like a green doll waving to the toy ships; New Jersey and my hometown were far off and winter brown. The most startling thing was to look straight down. From forty stories the world below looks very small and antlike. But from above seventy, the sidewalks, streets, cars, and people are infinitely smaller, mere poppy seeds moving about. The height is exaggerated by the way the lines of the building narrow in as your eye travels down the beams to the waiting ground below.

I was back on the building site the following two days, both times helping to haul away the mangled metal decking or moving equipment between floors. And I visited the towers as a tourist several times after they were completed, the last time with my family in June 2001. I know I always felt I was a part of the building's history, a very tiny part to be sure, but a part.

And now that building and its twin are gone. Destroyed before our eyes. When I recall that September day—the fiery explosions, the billowing smoke and rain of papers—when I think of the thousands of innocent lives wasted, the thousands more left grieving and empty, of the firefighters and police officers rushing into the buildings, even as pieces of metal were falling to the ground around them—a startling, frightening sadness comes over me. And rage.

Not so much rage at the people who planned and carried out the cowardly attack, or at their supporters who cheered the act, though, believe me, that is certainly there. The rage is more at my own helplessness and frustration. And at the way these recollections and emotions seem to surface at will these days, stopping cold whatever I happen to be thinking about or doing, to demand my attention and concern.

I've learned that I can't simply push the thoughts away and go on with my day. They will come back again and again to bother me. So I let those scenes replay themselves, let the feelings take hold again. There are even moments when I can picture myself inside the building moments before it collapses. The end is always the same—the floor suddenly drops away from under me and I am weightless a second, almost at peace, then I'm falling and the world is crashing in around me and I know there is nothing I can do.

It's that realization—that terrible things happen in life that can't be avoided or fixed—that lingers and nags me. And there's an endless list of questions, besides. Should we have seen these terrible deeds coming and been more prepared? Was there anything we could have done for the people inside the buildings, for the rescuers who went in? How is it that jealousy and hate can be wrapped in religious zeal and used to motivate murder? What can I do about any of this?

These and many other questions will be discussed and debated, publicly and privately, in the months and years ahead. There will be answers, and steps will be taken to help the families of survivors, to make our lives safer, to stop such crimes in the future. But, for all of this, I'm fairly certain we won't eliminate the sadness or anger. Not entirely, anyway.

As I've said, escaping these thoughts and feelings isn't possible. But I've learned how to slip past them, if only temporarily. I think about the towers when they were still in the process of being created—when the steel was new and the wind was the only thing challenging the structure.

It's then, too, that I recall my uncle Buddy most clearly, even to the change in his mood as we left the building site that day in 1970 and headed back to New Jersey. He still had some gruff words for the other foreman and for the elevator operator (who showed up just as we were preparing to leave, complaining about being rousted from bed at the ungodly hour of seven o'clock!). But Uncle Buddy's edginess was gone completely and he seemed pleased and happy—that no one had been hurt, and that we had gotten there fast and contained the problem before anything really bad had happened. The screwup would cost the construction company several thousand dollars, but it wouldn't delay any work at all (which would have cost tens of thousands of dollars).

I remember, also, some good-natured kidding about what I'd tell my mother about the emergency. "You mean about being eighty stories up on open steel?" I answered, knowing that this would set off my uncle, which it did. "Just kidding," I said, adding, "Oh, you mean the emergency at the Grace Building on the third floor?"

"It was the second floor," Uncle Buddy snapped out, "and don't go and forget it." Then he smiled. "Now let's go to the Tick Tock Diner and have some breakfast. I'm starved." And for a little bit of time I can remember and forget at the same time.

THREE CRISES

BY James Cross Giblin

September 11, 2001, was a perfect day for flying. In New York City the temperature was mild, a light breeze was blowing from the west, and the sky was a glittering blue without a cloud in sight.

Later, I would wish it had been rainy, or better yet foggy. Then maybe the hijackers' flights would have been delayed or canceled, and their murderous plot would have been foiled. But that morning I was glad it was sunny because I had plans for a little trip of my own. I was going up to Harlem to meet an author whose work I edited and look at photos she intended to use as illustrations in a future book.

I was deciding what to wear for the outing when the telephone rang, shortly before 9:00. It was my friend Ed. "Do you have the TV on?" he asked calmly.

"No. Why?"

"There's been an accident at the World Trade Center," he said, his voice still steady. "A small plane just crashed into it. I thought you'd like to know. It's on all the channels."

Hanging up, I switched on the set and saw smoke billowing from one of the twin towers. "The crash must have been caused by a navigational error," an announcer was saying.

I watched for a while, then phoned the author I was to meet later. She had her set on, too, and we spoke of the awful accident. But we decided not to let it stop us from going ahead with our plans.

Returning to the TV, I was just in time to see another plane—and not a small one—fly up to the second tower and disappear behind it. A moment later a huge ball of flame erupted from the tower. The plane I'd just seen must have plowed into it. With both structures hit, this was clearly no accident.

I phoned the author again and we shared our feelings— and our fears. "Do you think it's a terrorist attack?" she asked. "What else?" I said. "All those poor people . . ." she whispered, referring to those working on the towers' top floors where the planes had struck. We postponed our scheduled meeting, both of us realizing that travel around the city would be impossible in the wake of the attack.

I went back to the TV once more and, like millions of Americans and others around the world, watched incredulously as first one tower and then the other collapsed in an ominous mass of dust and smoke. Then word came of a similar attack on the Pentagon in Washington and the mysterious crash of yet another large passenger plane in a field in western Pennsylvania. By then, the familiar world I'd taken for granted a few hours earlier seemed to be threatened on all sides. I looked out my living room window and saw a corner of the Empire State Building, twelve blocks to the northwest. Would it be the attackers' next target?

After several hours of obsessive TV viewing and anxious phone calls from a stream of friends, I felt an urge to get away from the disaster. Besides, I needed a quart of orange juice and a loaf of bread, and guessed that the supply of both would soon be exhausted at the market across the street.

Outside on Third Avenue, I was reminded at once that this was no ordinary day. To the south, a swelling cloud of smoke from the fallen towers rose high in the sky and moved slowly east in the direction of Brooklyn. And along the sidewalk in front of me strode an unending stream of men and women dressed in their workaday best, many of them carrying briefcases. All public transportation to and from the Wall Street area had ceased, and most of the walkers were heading north, trying to get to their homes in upper Manhattan.

A few people were headed in the opposite direction. Two of them—a lanky, casually dressed man, and his seven- or eight-year-old son—approached me as I stood in front of my apartment house, waiting to cross the avenue. "How far is it from here to the Brooklyn Bridge?" the man asked me.

I thought for a second. "Probably about two miles," I said.

The boy looked worried. "That's a long way," he said, glancing up at his father.

"Not so long, really," the man said reassuringly. "Come along, Jeremy. We'll make it." He took his son's hand and they moved south along the sidewalk, bucking the oncoming crowd.

As I watched them go, my thoughts shifted abruptly to a different time, and a very different place: Sunday, December 7, 1941, in the living room of my family's comfortable old house in Painesville, Ohio. My mother and father were reading in their respective corners while I lay stretched out on the rug, drawing something—I don't remember what—in a spiral notebook. I was eight years old, about the same age as Jeremy, the boy I'd just seen.

From the radio in the corner came a symphonic piece played by the New York Philharmonic under the direction of the great conductor Arturo Toscanini. Suddenly a newscaster interrupted the music to announce, "A few minutes ago, at 7:55 A.M. local time, Japanese warplanes attacked the U.S. naval base at Pearl Harbor in the Hawaiian Islands."

My father and mother immediately stopped reading, and I put down my pencil. We listened silently as the announcer continued, "At least nineteen vessels, including eight battleships, have been sunk or severely damaged. Many lives have been lost, but the full extent of the casualties is not yet known. . . ."

Before the announcer had finished, my parents began to discuss the implications of the attack. "It means war, doesn't it?" my mother asked. "Yes, and not just with Japan," my father replied. "We'll probably have to deal with Hitler, too."

Without saying anything, I turned back to my notebook. But now I drew pictures of bombed-out buildings and houses, like photos I'd seen in *Life* magazine. They weren't of structures in far-off London or Rotterdam, though. Instead they were pictures of buildings I knew very well—Jackson Street School, where I was in third grade; the Cleveland Trust Bank Building, where my father had his law office; and our own house at 239 Mentor Avenue. I drew it with a big hole in the roof of the wing that contained my room.

That night before going to bed I asked, "Are we going to be bombed like those ships at Pearl Harbor?"

"I doubt it," my father said. "The Japanese are a long way away from Ohio. None of their planes can fly this far." He did his best to sound reassuring, but I could see a worried expression in his eyes and realized that he was upset, too. After he left, I kept shifting from one side to the other before I finally fell asleep.

The next morning I didn't want to go to school, but I got ready anyway. The school was only a short walk from my home, but that morning it seemed longer than usual. I kept looking up at the sky and listening for the distant roar of planes, even though I'd almost never seen a plane flying over Painesville.

At school I made a startling—and oddly comforting—discovery. Many of the other children were more scared than I was. Dick O'Neill, who was good at every sport, was sure the Japanese army would occupy our town. Della Poxon was so nervous she threw up her breakfast in the girls' room. Even Freddy Merrill, the class bully, was afraid that the school would be bombed and he would be killed.

Fortunately, our teacher, Miss Florence Littlejohn, knew just how to handle the situation. Miss Littlejohn seemed very old to us, although she probably wasn't more than fifty-five or sixty. And, most of the time, she scared us half to death with her fierce glare and thin-lipped expression when someone mis-behaved. But today she got us to talk about our fears, and even to laugh at some of the more far-fetched ones.

Once we began to relax, she surprised us even more by saying, "This morning, instead of starting as usual with our English lesson, how would you like to hear a story?"

"Yes, yes, Miss Littlejohn!" we chorused, and she went to the bookcase in the corner where she kept her supply of story-books. Our school didn't have a library—few elementary schools did in the 1940s, even in well-to-do suburbs—but Miss Littlejohn and a few other teachers maintained small classroom libraries of their own. Now she chose a thick volume from the bookcase and returned to her desk at the front of the room.

"This story is called *Heidi,* and it takes place in a far-off country called Switzerland," she told us. And for the next half hour or so, she transported us to the Swiss Alps and introduced us to Heidi and her grandfather, who were so happy in their mountaintop home with their flock of goats until Grandfather fell ill. . . .

"That'll be enough for today," Miss Littlejohn said at last. "Now we must get on with the English lesson." Reluctantly, we all left Switzerland and returned to our third-grade classroom. But something had changed. We still had our fears, but they didn't loom quite as large. Thanks to Miss Littlejohn, our spirits had been calmed, and we were ready to move ahead with our lives.

Memories of that long-ago Monday, December 8, 1941, lingered in my mind as I stood at the corner of Third Avenue, waiting for the light to change. The grocery store across the street was more crowded than I'd ever seen it, but I picked up a container of orange juice and grabbed one of the last loaves of bread: Pepperidge Farm's Cinnamon Swirl. Oh, well. It would make good toast.

While I waited in the long checkout line, a woman in a nearby aisle let out a scream when a display of cantaloupes suddenly toppled to the floor in an avalanche of fruit. "I'm sorry, I'm sorry!" the woman sobbed as one of the store workers hurried over to help her pick them up. "I didn't mean to do it," she wailed when one of the melons eluded her and rolled on across the floor. "I'm just so nervous, so upset by everything that's happened!"

Several of us in the checkout line exchanged sympathetic glances, and someone called out, "You're not alone, honey!" The line inched slowly forward, but the woman's words and the hysteria in her voice kept echoing in my head. I felt as if I'd heard them both before, but I couldn't figure out where or when. And then it came to me.

It was October 1962, the week of the Cuban missile crisis. By then, I'd been out of college for some years, and was the associate editor at a children's book publisher in New York City. When President John F. Kennedy announced that the Soviet Union was installing ballistic missiles in Cuba, tensions mounted throughout the United States. The president imposed a naval blockade on the island and warned that any missile launched from Cuba would be met with a retaliatory attack on the Soviet Union by the United States.

Even as Kennedy spoke, a fleet of Soviet ships loaded with more missiles was sailing toward Cuba. Many feared a nuclear war would be triggered if the ships tried to break through the U.S. blockade.

I was sure New York would be one of the first targets if war did come. To prepare for that awful possibility, I did something that even at the time seemed a little silly. I withdrew $500 from my bank account—a sum worth far more then than now—and hid it inside a book in my apartment. I figured it would be good to have a supply of cash on hand if I had to get out of the city quickly in the face of an imminent attack.

Meanwhile, I kept going to the office each day. As the week wore on, and threats and counter-threats were issued by both sides, that became harder and harder to do. Not just for me, but for everyone living in New York at the time. You could see the anxiety in people's eyes, hear the strain in their voices.

Things came to a head for me one morning late in the week when I was starting down the subway stairs to begin my daily commute to work. What happened wasn't grand in scale: a fire didn't break out in the tunnel, a train didn't derail. A well-dressed woman simply tripped and fell amid the crowd on the stairs. But it was enough to set off a scene. Before other riders, including me, could help the woman up, she cried out, "I can't go on! It's just too much. Today is the day—I know today is the day they're going to drop the bomb! We'll all be blown up, and I'll never see my family again!"

From down the track came the sound of a train approaching the station, but no one moved. Then an older woman broke the spell. "There's the train," she said. "Come on. We'd better get going."

By then, the woman was on her feet again, and her helpers were brushing off her suit. But she was still sobbing, more quietly now, as she stumbled forward with the crowd and boarded the train. Walking behind her, I realized that my legs were shaking. I, too, wondered if I'd be returning home that evening.

Three days later, on Sunday, October 28, the Soviet premier, Nikita Khrushchev, agreed to withdraw the Soviet missiles from Cuba and dismantle their launching sites. A confrontation had been avoided. The crisis was over. I was at a brunch with friends when word of the agreement came over the air, and we all heaved a tremendous sigh of relief. It was as if we'd been holding our breath for a week. On Monday morning, I re-deposited my $500 in the bank, and life in New York and the rest of the world gradually returned to normal.

Unfortunately, there was no such immediate relief from the crisis of September 11. Outside the grocery store, the crowd of pedestrians on Third Avenue had thinned. The sky above seemed an even deeper blue than in the morning. Gazing up at it and feeling the warm sun on my face, I could almost forget that the terrorist attack had ever happened. But not for long. One siren after another wailed in the distance, and when I looked down the avenue I could see the cloud of black smoke still rising from the ruined towers.

At that unsettling moment, I was grateful for my memories of Pearl Harbor and the Cuban missile crisis. Then, as now, we as a nation had been shaken out of our complacency and forced to confront a profoundly uncertain future. But, in the end, we'd survived, and found our way forward. That helped give me confidence that we'd be able to do so again.

As I walked into my apartment building, I thought of Jeremy and his father. By now they should be getting close to the Brooklyn Bridge; maybe they'd already started across it.

THE FALLING

BY AVI

It was not as if I wanted to kill anything. True, I was a twelve-year-old boy living in New York City, and more than anything I wanted a Red Rider air rifle. But just to make sure everyone understands, I need to say it again: I didn't mean to kill anything.

Consider: I was devoted to comic books, and virtually every issue that passed through my eager hands and beneath my all-believing eyes had a multicolored ad extolling the glories of a Red Rider rifle. It shot BB shot, but it was absolutely a Western rifle.

Who was Red Rider? He was a comic-book cowboy, and I would have liked to be one, bringing justice to the Old West, and along the way, becoming admired by girls. Clearly, however, you had to have a pump rifle to achieve all that.

To make that point very clear, Red Rider had a sidekick, a boy about my age—I was sure. I may be wrong, but I think his name was Rusty. He, too, had a rifle. Clearly a boy—like me—could solve lots of problems if he had such a weapon.

Besides, I lived in New York City. While it was true I rode the subways on my own, wandered the streets as I wished, went to the theater and ate Chinese food, the lure of the West was very great in those days.

If you had a rifle.

Now, for mere money I could buy my way into glory by purchasing a rifle with pump action that was so very much like the one Red Rider had.

I got one. I'm not exactly sure how it happened. Perhaps I saved up the money. I did have odd jobs, not the least of which was standing outside the nearest supermarket (small by today's standard) to wait for elderly ladies lugging big paper sacks, and saying, "Carry your package, Lady?"

If they said, "Yes," you did just that. Of course, you never knew how far you would have to go. There was no set fee. It was all tip money. It might be a dime. It could be as much as twenty-five cents.

Perhaps there was birthday money, too, or even Christmas coins from distant relatives.

In any case, I finally saved up enough money to buy an official Red Rider Pump Action BB Rifle.

Mind, it came about only after lengthy negotiations with my parents. Where would I use it? How? To what end? And of course, I must promise not to point it at anyone or kill anything.

Of course, I agreed to everything required.

Then I filled in a coupon, and got one of my parents to write a check and mail it all off.

Endless waiting followed. But I had been inured to such long waits by sending off for various decoder rings, cocoa mugs, and other radio hero items.

Then it came.

Of course, it was smaller than I thought it would be. And I had to put it together. I also had to purchase the BB shot separately.

All that was achieved.

Almost immediately, I began to break my promises about its use. I used the gun in my room—secretly. The BB pellets ricocheted wildly. My wallpapered room was soon as dimpled as a golf ball. I also shot out my window into a small backyard.

Fortunately, I didn't do any real damage. But then, my aim was terrible.

So, no harm done—not really.

Besides, it was fun.

Then, one day, my parents announced we would be spending a weekend in the country.

"Can I bring my gun?"

"You know the rules."

"I know."

"Then—as long as you use it away from the house and our friends—you can bring it."

"I promise."

We drove into the country with the rifle in the trunk, since it would be unsafe in the backseat with me. In time, we got to wherever we were going—I don't remember just where it was.

After the usual boring hellos, and how-do-you-dos—for the adults who had invited us—I was set free. With the rifle.

Moreover, I was delighted there were no other kids with whom I would need to share.

There was a large, open meadow behind these people's house. I asked for and received permission to take my rifle there.

"For target practice," I said.

"Have fun."

"Don't kill anything," someone else said.

"If you get a deer, we'll have him for dinner."

"Don't worry, he's not a good shot."

Paying no attention to the adult banter I walked out to the meadow, rifle in hand.

It was a lovely, late spring day. The sky was blue with just a few scattered clouds. The air was balmy. The grass was high. Swallows skimmed the golden tassels, darting here, there.

The question was: What should I aim at?

Then it happened.

A bird flitted across the meadow. I lifted my rifle, did a quick pump, aimed, and pulled the trigger.

I hit the bird.

To my utter astonishment it appeared to stop midflight. Its feathers ruffled. Its grace was gone. It plummeted straight down.

With it plunged my heart. And I was completely shocked.

That is to say, I had aimed at the bird, but that I actually hit it truly took my breath away.

This was many, many years ago, but I can see it now: the bird was tumbling. Its gravity-free grace was replaced by dead weight. Its very apparent weightlessness had been replaced by a leaden, lifeless fall.

I was horrified. Horrified to see the bird drop. Horrified to realize what I had done. And I was very frightened.

I had killed.

The bird fell perhaps thirty feet. Then just before it hit earth it miraculously righted itself, regained its sense of flying—and life itself—and flew away.

If I had been horrified one moment—what I now felt was enormous relief. It was as if the bird had been given another chance: a chance not to die. But, I was, too: a chance not to kill again.

· For a long while, I just stood there in the meadow, rifle in hand. I had been shaking. It took a long while to calm myself down, to relive what had happened over and over again.

Slowly, I walked out of the meadow back to the house. I opened the trunk of my parents' car, and dropped the Red Rider rifle in.

When I got home, I took that rifle apart. Day by day—secretly—I threw away each part.

When I witnessed—on television—the fall of the twin towers—I had a sudden and vivid recollection of that moment. This time, however, the bird did not rise.

DOORWAYS IN THE AIR

BY KYOKO MORI

On the morning of September 12, 2001, I woke up to the bleating call of the white-breasted nuthatch that was perched on a maple branch across the street from my fourth-floor apartment. *Whi-whi-whi*, he called as he soared up from the branch, flew across the street, and landed outside my window with a loud thump of his feet. Warily, he stared at my birdfeeder, which is an air-conditioner-sized box that sits on the sill. The opening of the feeder is the window itself, raised about seven inches. Birds have to come through that opening to the inside part of the windowsill to peck at the sunflower seeds and millet I put there. As they perch inside the feeder, the only thing separating them from me is the one-way mirror on the door of the feeder. I can see them, but they can't see me. Even so, few birds like to come so close to a big brick building like the one I live in. Nuthatches and chickadees—

another gray, white, and black bird—are the only ones who ever do.

This nuthatch lowered his head as though he had to duck and then hopped forward through the opening. He rummaged through the pile of sunflower seeds, picked one, and immediately flew out. After he returned to the branch across the street, he pounded the seed against the bark to crack it open, then swallowed the kernel. The next second, he was flying back toward my window. He landed, hopped through, picked another seed, and soared back to the tree. Back and forth he went for the next ten minutes, the pattern of his flight tracing graceful arcs, up and down, up and down, in the air between the tree and my window. He was connecting invisible dots and drawing pictures of doorways in midair—doorways suspended in the middle of nowhere.

My cats woke up just in time to see the nuthatch's last two or three rounds, before he had his fill and flew away. Crouched on the couch next to the window, the cats stared at the birdfeeder, hoping that the bird would return. The birdfeeder is a kind of cat TV. My cats watch the one-way mirror with the same scattershot attention people give their TVs when they are channel-surfing: their interest is perked up for a few seconds by something that looks good, but then the program quickly becomes boring, so they switch the channel or finally put down the remote control and walk away—or in my cats' case, they close their eyes and curl up for another nap.

That morning, I envied the cats their window-feeder TV in which nothing much happened except the occasional appearance of a nuthatch or a chickadee. Like millions of people across America, I had spent the previous day watching the same horrifying images over and over on my TV—not wanting to see them anymore, but afraid to leave. If I went away and came back, I thought, I might find new pictures on my TV, of other planes falling out of the sky, other towers on fire, in other cities across our country. By staying put in front of the screen, I was trying to prevent anything more from happening. Between the TV and the phone calls to and from friends to make sure that everyone we knew was safe, I felt like I was keeping a vigil late into the night. But now that I had been asleep for a few hours, I was afraid to turn the TV back on. Instead, I sat with the cats and stared at the empty birdfeeder.

It's been over a month since that morning. Outside my window, one maple tree has already shed its leaves while another, right next to it, is still green with just the tips touched in yellow. The nuthatch—the same one or maybe several different birds, I don't know—keeps coming back once or twice a day. When I think about the events of September 11, I'm torn between wanting to say nothing because no words can be enough—and wanting to describe everything that is still worth living for.

When I feel the second kind of urge, I think of the invisible doorways that the nuthatch continues to draw between the (now bare) tree and my window. I want to commit every flutter of his wings, every shake of his head, to memory. I don't have answers for the big questions: why does God, if there is a God, allow people to hate and kill one another; what is the point of going on and living a "normal life," whatever that is, when the world suddenly seems like such a dangerous place; why were some people killed and others spared when they were all innocent??? I will never have answers for these questions, though that doesn't mean they are not questions worth asking and thinking about.

As I contemplate these big questions, I want to keep my eyes on the invisible flight lines outside my window, the doorways opening to nothing except pure empty air. In spite of everything, I believe that there is a positive flow of energy in the universe. This energy is moving through the nuthatch as he shuttles between the tree and the window, as he soars up into the air and disappears till the next day. Perhaps the same force that moves the bird's wings is moving the hundreds of people who are still digging through the rubble of the World Trade Center and the Pentagon to find even the smallest traces of the people who had perished there; the same energy is flowing through still others who are raising money to help the survivors or organizing children across the country to write letters to the children in New York City.

Nothing we do will bring back the people who died or guarantee that no more acts of violence will hurt us. Everything we do is as "useless" as the nuthatch's flight, if by "useful," we mean having immediate, concrete results to make the tragedy go away. When the planes struck the World Trade Center and the Pentagon on September 11, I was at home writing. Several of my friends all across the country were also writing their stories, poems, or novels about ordinary people living ordinary lives and being comforted by the sight of blue hydrangeas blooming next to a hospital or by kind words exchanged between a mother and a daughter after a disagreement. For several days, weeks afterward, we wondered, What is the point of writing about such things any more? Why would anyone want to read any books? Should we now see and write about the world in a completely different way?

No doubt, some of us will come to address the big questions about peace and justice in our writing, more than we used to. I hope I will, too. But I still believe in writing about a perfect leaf as it falls from the tree, a small moment of understanding between people, or the blue wedges of light that fan across a lake on a cold winter day. By capturing these moments in words, we are drawing our own invisible doorways in midair, pointing a way to beauty or understanding—proving that just as surely as hatred exists between people, beauty also exists in the universe. This beauty, I am certain, will teach us to live in harmony with one another, with birds and trees and the sky, with everything there ever was.

For a long time after September 11, I thought that the world would never be the same again. We were now living in a dangerous place where anything could happen, where no one was ever safe. In a way, I still think that. I had never before lived in a place where—during my lifetime at least—buildings had been blown up and thousands of people killed at a stroke. In Cambridge, Massachusetts, four hours by car from New York, I am the closest I have ever been to a site of warlike destruction. Of course, I feel wary.

But this is not the first time I've lived in a place that had been demolished by war—if I include events from before I was born. Until I was twenty, I lived in Kobe, Japan, a city that was rebuilt after the Second World War. When my mother was fifteen, she and her family saw bombs falling from the sky and burning up their neighbors' houses, destroying the downtown shopping district where they used to buy books and clothes, and reducing to rubble the pharmacy that belonged to their relatives. Years later, when my cousins and I—all of us born long after the war ended—complained about having to stand in line, to eat food we didn't like, or to do some chore we wished we could skip, my mother, uncles, aunts, and grandparents smiled indulgently but insisted that we were spoiled, that we had no idea what real suffering was. They didn't tell us many details about exactly what they had endured, perhaps because they did not want to scare us or because their memories were too painful. They only mumbled a few words about being afraid of firebombs or having nothing to eat. My cousins and I turned up our noses and rolled our eyes, thinking, "Here they go again, talking about the war." Like everything else that happened before we were born, the war seemed to us like an old story.

Now, as I step out of my apartment building and walk in my neighborhood in America—a country that has been my country for the last twenty-four years—I remind myself that all through my childhood in Japan, I was walking where buildings had burned to the ground. By the late fifties and early sixties, when I was a child, my hometown had been rebuilt completely. There were many neighborhoods where a few old wooden houses stood surrounded by modern buildings. I knew that this odd mixture of building styles had something to do with how the firebombs had struck some houses but not all. Those few old houses were the only things left from before the war, and the new buildings had been built around them. But I didn't realize that my mother, who walked beside me, might have been remembering the houses that used to be on that street when she was a young girl, or the people who used to live there—some of whom, I know now, must have perished in the bombings.

My mother kept holding my hand and walking with me, guiding me through the neighborhood of her childhood— pointing out a pretty flower here, a singing bird there, a funny dog on someone's lawn—while her mind must have wandered now and then to the destruction she had witnessed a long time before. My uncles and aunts were doing the same thing in their neighborhoods with my cousins. They had all seen different versions of what I saw on TV over and over since September 11, and then they lived on and became our parents and loved us and taught us about beauty and patience and kindness.

One of the few things my mother told me about the war was that afterward, she had to change her views about the world: during the war, she had been taught, like all the schoolchildren of Japan, that the Japanese emperor was God and that the expansion of the Japanese empire into the rest of Asia was a glorious, good plan. After the war, she learned about the terrible things Japanese soldiers had done to innocent people in China, Korea, and all over Asia. She felt ashamed when she recalled the rallies she had attended at school in support of the war. She had to take stock of what had really happened and promise herself that she would never support war and violence.

The terrorists' attacks on New York and Washington, D.C., on September 11 are not the same as the war my mother and her family experienced in Japan in the 1940s. America was not at war in September 2001. The people who were at the World Trade Center and the Pentagon, the people who boarded the planes that were hijacked, and the police officers and the firefighters who died on duty had not been supporting war or cruelty as my mother had been taught to do in Japan sixty years before, though perhaps that is what the terrorists would have us believe. For those of us left here, though, we are just as bewildered as my mother must have been as a young woman. We don't know why our country was attacked. We don't know what—if anything—we could have done to prevent the tragedy.

But maybe feeling confused is a good beginning. Confusion can lead to questions—big questions, good questions. Now is our chance to think about how we should live in a world that will never be the same. I don't have answers for the big questions about how to bring about world peace—whether, on the way to peace, we need to wage war against those who oppose it. Still, I know that the tragedy has brought me finally into the same community of suffering and survival that my mother and her family had belonged to. It's the same community that most of the rest of the world had belonged to before September 11. Had I been born elsewhere, I might have seen bombs and land mines, soldiers and tanks, famines and epidemics every year of my life. Having grown up in Japan after the war and then moving to the United States, I had been lucky: I had been sheltered from the war, violence, and hunger that devastated a great portion of the world. Before the events of September, I had been living in an oasis of peace that was the United States, an oasis of unusual safety by the standard of the world. Even as I grieve the loss of our oasis, I want to welcome the opportunity to belong to the rest of the world. Perhaps that is the only way I can embrace the flow of energy in the universe: in the flight of the nuthatch, in the stories my mother told me, in the bond that suffering creates between people past and present, here and there, and all over the world.

SISTER

BY SUSAN COOPER

I was in Manhattan on September 11, 2001, in our uptown apartment. The radio was on. My husband and I heard the news of the first plane hitting the World Trade Center, then the second, and we went up to the top of our 49-story building and looked out, numb, at the smoke pouring into the sky from the two towers. When we went back to our apartment, the radio—whose transmitter had been on top of the Trade Center—was broadcasting nothing but static. We turned on the television set, and saw the images of the two towers collapsing. And after that, of course, the terrible unthinkable earlier images of the planes flying into the buildings: the images none of us will ever forget.

Because everyone in New York thought there would be thousands of wounded people needing blood transfusions, we went out into the street to find a hospital where we could give blood. By then all the airports had been closed, and also all the bridges and tunnels leading in and out of New York, so the streets were almost empty of traffic, the sky empty of planes. Smoke was hazing the air to the south. Then suddenly there was a roar as a U.S. fighter plane flew over the city, and I stood still, frozen, because the sound had taken me instantly back to my childhood, to another time of defense and attack.

When I was a child, in England, World War II was going on. We lived twenty-three miles outside London, near the main railway line to the west, and because the enemy bombers were always trying to hit the railroad, we were often under attack. It was normal. We had never known a time without war, my brother and me. The government had issued big curved sheets of galvanized steel to every family with a garden, and our father had dug a big hole in the lawn and made an air-raid shelter, its entrance protected by sandbags, its roof covered by earth and grass. We would go to bed at night knowing that sooner or later the air-raid siren would start its up-and-down wail and our parents would wrap us in coats and rush us down into the shelter, where we would sit listening to the chatter of the antiaircraft guns at the end of the road, and the dull thumps of approaching bombs, and sometimes the roar of low-flying planes. We had one candle burning, and its flame would shake with each thump.

The planes were German, of course, because we were at war with Germany. And in Germany, other children in other air-raid shelters were listening with exactly the same emotions to the noise of other planes, and of British and, later, American bombs.

We walked to school every morning with a schoolbag over one shoulder and a gas mask over the other, and once we arrived to find a huge bomb crater at the edge of the playground, and another where a house next to the school had been.

You could find bits of shrapnel scattered about after a bomb had exploded, and there was always a strong smell of dust, and of burning.

New Yorkers got to know that smell, after September 11, 2001.

I met my first American when I was walking to school one day, halfway through the war. He was sitting on a tank, where a convoy of tanks and guns and trucks had stopped on the road, and he smiled at me. Perhaps I reminded him of another small girl 4,000 miles away, at home. "Hey, sister," he said, and he gave me a candy bar. I took it very cautiously, and then I ran away. I hope I said thank-you.

Sister.

When you live in a country that is at war, and under attack, you discover—all of you—a sense of community that was not there before. It's as if your family has suddenly grown, to embrace everyone in the country—including, in our case, foreign soldiers, sailors and airmen sent from abroad to fight on our side.

People in this great extended family become more understanding, more tolerant, even under stress. "We're all in this together," they say to each other. They help other people not to be afraid. They do small generous things, like giving a child a candy bar, or huge heroic things, like pulling bomb victims out of collapsing buildings, driving ambulances through machine-gun fire, or waiting on exposed roofs to put out firebombs when they fall.

There were hundreds of heroes in New York and Washington, and up in airplanes, on September 11, 2001, and many of them are dead. War was declared on the United States by terrorists that day. Their intention was to damage not just individual people, but the spirit of the nation. They wanted to spread fear. It is the business of terrorists to create terror, if they can.

But the opposite of terror is hope, and if the sense of family can remain strong across this country, hope can drive out fear. It's not easy: this is a very big and diverse nation. Each one of us needs to remember that story about the bundle of sticks, which is unbreakable so long as it is a bundle, but can easily be broken stick by stick if it comes apart. Alone, we may be afraid. Together, we can have hope.

A week after September 11, 2001, I was asked to write a poem for a concert to benefit the victims of the disaster—though it wasn't so much a concert as a gathering, at which performers and audience all sang together, for comfort, for remembrance, for tomorrow. Perhaps the poem I wrote has a connection with what I've been trying to say here, and with the intention of this book. Here it is:

SEPTEMBER 11, 2001

*The workers falling from the World Trade Center included a man and
a woman holding hands.*

—New York Daily News

So darkness came, and changed the sunlit world,
Blind hatred blasting thousands into dust,
Filling the sky with flame and pain and death
And one doomed couple falling hand in hand.

Honor their image, for those two linked hands
Contain the power to drive the dark away:
He is my brother, though I do not know him;
She is my sister, though I do not know her,
Together we preserve humanity.

All hands link now, to save and to console,
To mend, to guard, to love and to avenge
(Though eye for eye would blind the human race).
Evil will fall into its own cold doom
When nations of all races and beliefs
Go hand in hand, to heal this altered world.

ASKING WHY? WHY? WHY?

Our Persistent Struggle to Understand

ASKING WHY? WHY? WHY?

How can we understand the events of 9/11? The difficulty in answering that question is acknowledged by Nikki Giovanni in the sparely eloquent poem that begins this section. Marc Aronson and Marina Budhos then explore the complexity of issues and emotions that present an answer, set on the stage of world history, to why "it" happened and why now. Virginia Euwer Wolff offers a story told in the voices of a trio of young musicians who look for answers and understanding in the orderly, contrasting, complicated, and harmonious sounds of music. And Suzanne Fisher Staples takes us to the shadow of a persimmon tree in Pakistan's Northwest Frontier province, where Afghan refugee children assemble to study, to ask questions, and perhaps, to find answers.

DESPERATE ACTS
(FOR 9/11)

BY NIKKI GIOVANNI

It's not easy to understand
Why angry men commit
Desperate acts

It's not easy to understand
How some dreams become
Nightmares

Those who wish
And those who need
Often feel alone

It's easy to strike back
But it's hard to understand

WHY? WHY? WHY?

BY MARC ARONSON AND MARINA BUDHOS

We can ask why three thousand times, and more, for every person killed in the attacks on September 11, for every family ripped apart, for every plan and hope and dream destroyed. We don't have any idea how to answer those tragic questions. But there is another kind of why question that we can begin to answer: why did it happen? Why now? What is going on in the world, in the year 2001, that would lead to such destruction? That is what history can do for us: it can help us to understand.

    Something new was taking place at the very end of the last century: for the very first time in human history there was one nation that dominated the entire planet, and that was, and is, the United States. We are by far the largest economy; we have the strongest armies; we have the most influence over other nations. There have always been strong nations and empires, but until the sixteenth century, those in the Old and New World did not even know of each other's existence. And even in the nineteenth century when, as it is said, the sun never set on the British Empire, England had powerful rivals such as Germany that were comparable in strength. Since the fall of communism in the Soviet Union in 1989, the United States has had no peer. While China has a huge population, a growing economy, and a powerful army, it neither has strong influence on nations outside of Asia nor seeks to have that power.

There is also something strange and different about how the United States dominates the world. Unlike, say, Genghis Khan, who controlled more land area than any other conqueror, or Queen Victoria, whose colonies stretched over Africa, Asia, Australia, and even the Caribbean, America does not exert its power primarily through rule. Americans do not serve as presidents of other nations or generals of their armies. Instead, American power—though ultimately backed by military forces—comes through business and through the media. America does not as much send its soldiers overseas as it does its companies and managers, its movies, CDs and TV shows, its advertisements and Internet links.

No matter where you are in the world, you will soon enough come in contact with American sodas and cigarettes, American sports events and soap operas, American jeans and banner ads. If you are eager to buy these things, but cannot afford to; or are prevented from doing so by the policies of your own government; or you do not want to, if they seem alien to you, America may well seem like a kind of disease, a poison, spreading into your world. America as it comes through the TV screen may seem like a siren in an ancient myth, something that calls to you, offering sweets but actually bringing your destruction.

Imagine a village, an ancient village where people have farmed and lived among one another for centuries, marrying, bearing children, carrying on with age-old rituals. At night they gather around and sing songs, tell traditional stories. Suddenly a TV is bought in one house. The homes go quiet and dark as everyone gathers around the blue-lit screen flashing with alien places and strange lives, far removed from their own. The old songs, the old ways, are forgotten; the songs seem to die in the people's throats; the children chant tunes from Barney.

Or a twisting lane in a big old city, where the women's long dresses whisper against the dirt; where men smile and hold hands; where everyone knows the rules and codes of behavior. Then it begins with small things: bars of soap, Pond's face cream, too expensive to buy; books, videos crammed with car crashes and blood spurting and terrible violence. Or there are the new shiny stores lined up on the boulevard, filled with televisions and jeans that cost a whole month's salary. They seem to leer, to remind you of how small, how inconsequential you are, how forgotten are the blue-tiled roofs of your ancient city. Every day you wait in line for simple things: water, a working telephone, someone to clear away the garbage; every day you learn of a country far off where everything runs smoothly, but it gives vast amounts of money to those government officials who make you sit and wait and feel humiliated, those police who beat and torture behind closed doors. Your country, your land, so steeped in history and tales, is falling behind; the boys line up outside the consulate, to leave, never to come back. Every time they leave it is a small rip in your self-esteem; a feeling that there is nothing here anymore to keep them.

Then there are boys who do return, their shoulders hunched, their eyes guarded, who speak with tight lips about their time, over there. The shabby rooms they lived in, the hard stares, the doors shut, the infidel men and women, laughing behind their golden-lit houses. The boys who cannot, despite years and years of school, find a job, even a small one. Whose eyes become veiled in hate; who listen to the soothing words of a leader who tells them why their lives are so dead, why so much has been taken from them. They sit in dusky cool corners, in cafes, reciting, bringing up the old phrases and prayers and songs that were almost forgotten; their chests fill with purpose; they swagger now. The words that are soft and lapping are soon hard, bunched like muscles, a fist, something to smash that place, that TV, those blond women with long thighs, those greedy, selfish people who will not let you alone, nor let you in.

It swells, this hatred; it cleanses, stronger than the hottest of baths; it pleases you through the dark days when the ceiling drips, or your father is humiliated in front of an official, or you must endure another no from an employer, or the rats scuttle in garbage black and gummy as tar. Even when life is good, when you have a job and your wallet sits fat against your hip, it gives you the feeling that you are part of something greater; you have seen the power shimmering off the ancient cobblestones, a force that will tear down to rubble that flimsy sham of a country, with its paper-thin morals, its shallow people. You are better and you know it. You and all around you will one day triumph.

This anger at America is sometimes cynically exploited by weak rulers and frightened elites who are themselves able to enjoy the best this country has to offer, but who whip up resentment toward the United States to distract the mass of people from their own frustrations. Some may experience these emotions just because they are envious sorts of people, as we all are at times—

feeling it is unfair that others have what we want, and then deny- ing that we wanted it in the first place. Still others may see aspects of the America they see or hear about that they simply do not like—sexual permissiveness, women working outside the home, great inequality between rich and poor, racial conflict, disrespect between the generations, even perhaps the fact that Christianity is the dominant religion, or that Jews are respected and prominent. Whatever the source of this distaste for America, it can go in a number of directions. Some people write books criticizing the country or its policies. Some join protests. Some try to move away into self-contained communities. Others look for more destructive ways to act.

America, its images, its music, its ways of doing business, can seem so dominant that those who want to resist it must often feel quite helpless, and they look for ways to shore up their own sense of power. They may turn to faith, thinking that a higher power will come to their aid. They may seek others with similar views, to form a band that finds strength in numbers. And they will look for ways to act. Plotting and planning to bring harm to America—and then actually doing so—must give those who oppose America a great feeling of accomplishment. They have struck back against the giant, and drawn blood.

If you think of all the stories we so often tell about heroic underdogs—David against Goliath, Luke Skywalker against the Empire, Frodo and the Fellowship against the armies of Mordor, the Minutemen against the Redcoats—it is not hard to imagine how America's enemies view themselves.

We are, then, paying a price for being so dominant. Is there any sense in which we are at fault? This is debated. Some would claim that specific policies of ours have been flawed and

helped spark some of this resentment—how can we be so dominant when we are responsible for overthrowing popular regimes,
or favoring corrupt governments, or supporting countries, such
as Israel, that others detest? But it is also true that if you live in
a country that is not doing terribly well economically, has had
little or no political freedom, is falling behind in technology,
and science, and medicine, it is easier to build up fury at
America than to try to change conditions at home. Callous governments and citizens frightened of repression agree that anger
at America is justified; anger at those same rulers is forbidden.

There is one sense, though, in which it is clear that we
are paying a kind of price for our success. We have long known
that there were individuals, organizations, and governments around
the world that could not stand the kind of world America
seemed to be leading and creating. While we have enjoyed the
benefits of being in touch with the whole world, we have too long
ignored what we knew. We did not feel it was necessary, essential,
to get in touch with our enemies, to persuade them to change
their views if possible, to contain their aggression if necessary.
We simply pretended they were not there, filing away on dusty
shelves endless reports about their beliefs and activities. We
wanted access to the entire world without taking full responsibility for the collisions, irritations, tensions that that could produce.
We were willfully blind, and in the darkness those whose hatred
had been burnished into a sharp weapon were free to act.

Why? Because if we are—and we certainly are—the most
dominant country in the world, we must also be the most aware.
We have to be in touch with the rest of the world, not simply
visitors who stop in to buy and sell, or images on a screen, or
sounds from a boom box. To be truly global is to be in contact
with everyone, so that we know where pockets of hatred are rising,

or where need is turning to desperation, or ignorance to violence. The obligation of our success is communication. The thousands of deaths on September 11 are a terrible price to pay for what can seem such a simple truth. But at least if we come away from this tragedy with a sense that there is something we can do, and must do—learn one another's languages, listen to one another's music, pay attention to one another's leaders and policies, study one another's faiths, be, together, citizens of the world—then it will have, at a great price, helped us to move on to the future.

Perhaps in ten, or twenty, or fifty, or one hundred years when we ask why, why did it happen, we, or our children, or their children, will say: because everyone was just beginning to learn that they shared a planet, and had to live together as attentively, as thoughtfully, as observantly as all members of the same family. If they do say that, they will also thank those who gave up their lives to teach us the one lesson living on earth demands of all of us.

BACH. BEETHOVEN. BRAHMS.
A SKETCH FOR VOICES

BY Virginia Euwer Wolff

People who make music together can't be enemies. At least not while the music lasts.

—Paul Hindemith

Terry, age 11
When the planes hit the buildings and everything got changed, I was afraid and I didn't know what to do. Partly because I'm only a kid, partly because school got out early and everybody had to go home, and partly because—I don't really know exactly why—I went to Bach. The Preludio no. 17 in E-flat major. The whole piece is in groups of threes, and the pattern going up and down the piano keys helped take my mind off the horrible, scary explosions. The music is so orderly, with a place for every note

and every note in its place, and it swells and calms down over and over again, and the way the notes go together made my brain get some balance. Finding that my fingers and the patterns of the music actually fit together was the only thing that made sense that day. Just three years ago I couldn't have played this piece. I couldn't have read the notes and kept looking down at my fingers and up again at the page fast enough. The smoke, the flames, the panic. And I'm just a kid, what could I do? I played and played.

Dana, age 14
Nothing in my life had prepared me for the explosions and people screaming and buildings burning and falling. I didn't have any words, and I kept sputtering questions. School was out early. My normal home looked abnormal. I couldn't stop thinking of the people in the airplanes, suddenly knowing they were going to die. People doing their jobs in their offices. Kids with no parents coming home. The fires, the fear, the screams. I went to Beethoven. By some kind of instinct. His Sonata no. 8 in C Minor, the *Pathétique*. My teacher wouldn't even let me play it till this year, because my hands couldn't reach the octaves with any room to spare. With Beethoven, the sound itself keeps changing its mind. Aggressive, ferocious, bruising—and then it can turn into lightly flowing silk. Small black notes on a page, my eyes reach to them and send commands to my brain, the messages pass through my synapses to my hands, and the ends of my fingers press on the keys and cause the hammers to hit inside the piano, making waves of different frequencies, to turn into tumult and whispers. The physical work of bringing this force of sound up out of the piano was a relief in itself. I still kept seeing the burning buildings in my mind, but I had to keep concentrating on the music—the loudest and softest, the heaviest and lightest. Storm and calm,

that's Beethoven. He composed it in C minor; they say it was his key of fate. I kept playing. I don't know how long. I just didn't stop and didn't stop.

Pat, age 17

The unspeakable horror, the shattered lives of so many thousands of people made my brain cells hurt, as well as every bit of emotional fiber I have. School was out early, everybody scattered, nearly incoherent with shock and grief and rage. And no sense to be made of any of it. The questions multiplied, the answers were nowhere. I looked at my house: floor, walls, and ceilings in their places. The piano my parents are making payments on, exactly where it was when I left for school early in the morning. As if the attack hadn't happened. But it couldn't not have happened. I went to Brahms, his short pieces, some Intermezzi, op. 117 and 118. Brahms. The layers of rhythm, the key changes, the astonishing harmonies and complicated chains of notes that lead to feelings lodged somewhere so deep that I don't even remember I have them most of the time. Brahms and his gigantic extremes, from the softest love to torment to exultation. You even have to have big hands to play this music. No matter how many times I shake my head and try to say it was a bad dream, I know it wasn't. It did happen and we're all changed and we don't even know how yet. I never had to feel so terribly, terribly sorry for the world before. I kept playing, the glowing sections and the grieving sections merging into each other. My hands sometimes not fast enough, my mind not big enough to contain all of this. It's private music, and I played it in private.

Terry

Bach's music shows me there's a way to make sense of this horrifying confusion. It doesn't tell exactly how, but the music gives hints that chaos won't last forever. Kind of like the arch of a bridge across a river. It's a solid curve and it goes a long, long way across. Bach was born in 1685, when violent religious wars were happening in Europe. The music he composed by candlelight has been lifting people up out of despair for more than three hundred years.

Dana

Bach had been dead for two decades when Beethoven was born. It was a time of revolutions, the Napoleonic wars. With Beethoven, you know the world is going to be disrupted. Cold loneliness and ugliness and death are real and you can't avoid them. He even makes you linger over them. But there's a grim kind of hope, too, that the human mind can look at the worst and not give in. Face it and not cringe.

Pat

Brahms was born six years after Beethoven died. He lived through the nineteenth century, with all its wars and diseases, and he was still alive to see the adding machine, the telephone, the electric stove, the photograph, and the automobile. A piano has only eighty-eight keys, but he used them to bask in sorrow and tragedy, and afterward you still feel bad, but the music is so beautiful and heartbreaking, it makes room for the sadness. More room than I thought I had inside.

Terry
Bach for balance when everything has gone crazy.

Dana
Beethoven for strength and courage. A furious will to live.

Pat
Brahms: music to let a grown man cry.

Dana
What do you think would happen if they got all the enemies together, in one room, and they had them listen to music—

Terry
All day long—

Pat
For as long as it takes. Days. Weeks.

Dana
How could they listen to that much music and still want to kill each other?

Pat
They couldn't. Could they?

Terry, Dana, Pat
What do you think?

UNDER THE PERSIMMON
TREE: A SHORT STORY

BY Suzanne Fisher Staples

Every morning seven Afghan refugee children assemble under the shade of a persimmon tree in a garden in Peshawar in Pakistan's Northwest Frontier to study multiplication, division, and the heavenly bodies.

"You must come every day," Bibi Nusrat tells the children, who fidget and squirm, "or you will never be anything but refugees when this war is over." Away from the noise and dust of the refugee camps Bibi Nusrat, who is American, talks to the children about the poetry of numbers each morning. Afternoons they talk about the dance of the planets and stars in the expanding universe.

They sit side by side on three rope cots that their teacher has drawn into a U-shape in the shade of the tree. It's autumn, and when a persimmon falls with a juicy plop in the weedy grass, the children scramble after it. Farooq retrieves it and eats its puckery custard quickly, without sharing. Wali takes advantage of the interruption to snatch Amina's scarf from her head. Bibi Nusrat thinks of the pears she and her brothers ate from the tree on her grandfather's farm near Watertown, New York, when she was a child. But she has acquired a taste for persimmons.

The children were shepherds in Afghanistan, and the boys in particular have difficulty sitting in one place for more than a few minutes. They arrive each day hungry, having had only tea at home. Every morning their mothers leave them at Bibi Nusrat's and rush to the bazaar, where they stand in line waving their ration cards over their heads. There is no shortage of food in Peshawar, despite the drought—but the refugees have no money.

Bibi Nusrat, who is wealthy only by the standards of Peshawar, believes education is as essential as eating. She reels in the children like fish, luring their bodies with food and their spirits with stories about the stars. It's their minds she's after.

Farooq and Farid—brothers—first came to Bibi Nusrat's kitchen in early spring, when the sweet peas climbed the strings hung from the garden wall, their pale lavender fragrance drifting through the open shutters. Bibi Nusrat's Pashtu was not as good then, and she thought they'd come to study, as she'd arranged with Haroon, the *malek* of the Shahnawaz Refugee Camp. The truth is the boys' mother had heard a rich foreigner lived in the house beside the persimmon tree, and they'd come looking for food. Bibi Nusrat promised to feed them if they'd stay and learn their numbers.

Bibi Nusrat's husband, Faiz ul-Haq, has gone off to fight the Taliban, and she misses him with a physical pain, as she would miss a severed arm or leg. She doesn't allow herself to think about missing Faiz except in the evenings, when she lies on

her back in the garden and looks at the stars. She was born
Elaine Perrin in New York, a girl who grew up wanting to help
people. When she married, Faiz had named her Nusrat, which
means "help." Teaching the refugee children in her garden, she
felt she'd earned her name.

Farooq and Farid were followed by Fariel, whose father
had been killed by the Taliban, her mother left a young widow
with three children. Then came Amina and her sister Tahira. The
class moved then from the kitchen to the garden, where there was
more room under the persimmon tree. Next came Ahmed and
his brother Wali. Bibi Nusrat guessed the children were aged
between eight and eleven, but age was something shepherds
seemed to care little about.

Bibi Nusrat puts away the board with the three-times
table on it and signals toward the open kitchen window at the
back of her plaster-walled house. Husna, a dark-eyed servant
woman in a faded blue tunic, scurries out with a heavy tray held
awkwardly in front of her. Bibi Nusrat drags a rough wooden
table into the space in the center of the wood-and-string cots
and Husna sets the tray on it. She takes the plates of kebabs and
naan and fruit and seven tumblers of filtered water from the tray
and places them on the table.

Meanwhile, the children crowd around a painted metal
stand that holds a basin of water beside the kitchen door. They
nudge each other aside to scrub their hands, drying them on a
worn pink towel before coming to the table. Bibi Nusrat passes
them the plates and they grab for the spicy meat patties and the
still-warm bread, jostling each other in a chaotic ritual they per-
form day after day.

As the children eat and talk noisily, with chickens
scratching for crumbs under the cots, Bibi Nusrat's eye drifts

over to a movement beyond the top of the garden wall. Neatly folded black turban pleats glide back and forth in a space of several feet just beyond the metal garden gate. Unnoticed by the children, she walks quietly to the gate and peers over its top.

A tall, slender boy whirls when he senses someone is watching. The embroidered tail end of his black turban is clamped firmly between his teeth. Bibi Nusrat regards him carefully. He is perhaps ten or eleven years old. His eyes are large—they're outlined carefully in black *surma*—and his mouth is wide, showing even white teeth clamped on the edge of the turban. Head to foot, clothing and skin, he is the color of dust.

"*A-salaam-alei-kum*," says Bibi Nusrat. "Please come in," she adds, holding the gate open for him. "Are you hungry?" She gestures toward the rough wooden table where the other children have stopped their gnawing to turn and stare at the new arrival, who stands just beyond the open gate. The boy's eyes flicker over the plates and linger on the kebabs. "Have some," says Bibi Nusrat. "If you've come to study, you can't do it on an empty stomach."

He glides through the garden as if he's drawn on a stream of air, and Bibi Nusrat thinks, This child also is a shepherd. His feet seem barely to touch the ground, and his eyes never leave the plates of food. Bibi Nusrat leads him to the table.

The others watch as he eats hungrily, without bothering to sit. He watches them back over a second kebab. Husna fetches him a tumbler of water from the earthenware filter urn on a table in the corner of the garden. He lowers his eyes only when she hands him the water. When he is finished Bibi Nusrat hands him the damp pink towel to wipe his hands and mouth.

"What's your name?" Bibi Nusrat asks. "Would you like more?"

He shakes his head and says, "Shaheed. I am Shaheed." The name means "martyr."

Bibi Nusrat notices something else about Shaheed. Unlike most of the children in the camp, his clothes are new. His tunic and trousers are rolled at the cuffs and his toes are hidden inside his sandals. Most refugee children wear clothing that has been handed down several times. They wear everything until it is more holes than fabric or until it covers so little it must be passed on to the next smaller child.

"Are you here to learn numbers?" she asks. He blinks and doesn't answer immediately. "Would you like to sit down?" She gestures to the wooden cots, which already spill over with children, two filled with boys and one with girls. Shaheed watches Bibi Nusrat intently, and he backs slowly until his legs hit a cot, forcing him to sit suddenly in a space vacated when Farooq and Ahmed scoot apart to make room.

The wind gusts. Dust flies into their faces, leaving their teeth gritty. It also has grown colder and the sky is an angry blue-gray. While Husna clears the lunch and drags the table away, Bibi Nusrat carries the old easel with the chalkboard on it to the open space at the head of the U and taps it with her pointer.

"This afternoon," she begins, "we will talk more about time and space. Last week we talked about a star that exploded 160,000 monsoons ago. The star was so far away that we're just now seeing the explosion. Does anyone have a question?" Amina stands.

"Uncle says this is wrong," she says so quietly Bibi Nusrat can barely hear her. "He says this is an un-Islamic idea."

"It is neither an Islamic idea nor an un-Islamic idea," says Bibi Nusrat. "It is science. The Koran came long before people knew these things about time and distance in the heavens. People invented myths to explain what they couldn't understand. Do you remember what myth is?"

Wali jumps up and down in his seat. "Yes, Wali?" says Bibi Nusrat.

"Myth is a story, like the story about the demon star that is the eye of the monster with snakes in her hair," he says proudly. Wali loves the star stories.

"Yes," says Bibi Nusrat, "the star is called 'demon' because its light is unpredictable—it is a story invented to explain what was otherwise unexplainable."

Just then a gust of wind blows the chalkboard over, and when Bibi Nusrat rights it, the wind topples it again. The children take advantage of the disturbance and begin laughing and shoving at each other. Shaheed draws himself in, as if to keep from touching the boys beside him. To add to the confusion, large drops of rain plat into the dust of the garden, and the children help Bibi Nusrat drag the cots under the shelter of the stoop outside the kitchen door before running for home in the refugee camp.

"Remember division," Bibi Nusrat calls after them. "I'll ask you about division first thing tomorrow. Chicken for dinner— and I will tell you another star story!" She turns to hurry inside as the wind pushes the rain so hard it stings her face. She nearly collides with Shaheed, who stands under the shelter of the kitchen stoop, his hands clasped in front of him.

"I need somewhere to sleep," he says, his face coloring deeply, his eyes widening. He clasps his hands tightly, as if to keep them from flying away. "I work hard. I can help out."

Bibi Nusrat leads him away from the driving rain, through the kitchen into the sitting room at the front of the house. A horse pulls a wooden cart past the front gate outside the window, its hooves squelching in the already muddy street. She gestures to a chair with horsehair stuffing and cotton batting visible through the worn damask on its seat. Shaheed looks at the chair dubiously and sits facing the window. Bibi Nusrat pulls up a wooden chair to sit in front of him so she can look into his face.

Bibi Nusrat reaches to a bowl on the table in front of the window and picks up a bright orange persimmon that sits on top of a pyramid of ripe fruit, and places it in the palm of Shaheed's hand. The persimmons are ripening rapidly, and she can barely give them away quickly enough.

"Where are your family?" she asks Shaheed.

"Dead," he says. "I came alone from Kunduz." The fighting has been heavy in Kunduz, with American jets carpeting the ground with bombs. The numbers in the refugee camps have swelled as the bombing increases, and everyone says no civilians remain in Kunduz.

"The Taliban forced my father and older brother to go with them," says Shaheed, looking at her directly. "We heard they died in Kandahar." He begins to turn the persimmon over and over in his fingers. "The last thing he said to my mother as he was taken away was that she should stay, no matter what happens. He was afraid they'd take our house, our land, and our sheep."

"And did she? Stay?" He nods and looks around the room before speaking, as if to be certain no one else is there. He keeps turning the persimmon in his fingers.

"She and my little brother were running to the house. I was in the doorway. We couldn't hear the airplanes for the bombs, but the earth was jumping all around us. I shouted at them to run faster. Then, suddenly, I was on the ground, covered with dirt. The house was gone except for the doorway, which still stood over me. I couldn't see my brother. My mother sat in the dirt close to where I'd been standing. I began to crawl toward her. She put out her hand and opened her mouth to speak. But instead of words, blood poured from her mouth. She was already dead."

Bibi Nusrat sits very still while she listens to Shaheed speak of his family and the terrible things that happened to them. He tells her about putting on his brother's new clothes, walking with a family from a nearby village to the border crossing, and hitching a ride to Peshawar on a truck filled with apples.

"Where have you been sleeping?" she asks. A deep pink spreads across Shaheed's cheeks and creeps down his neck.

"I crawled into a fruit stall in the bazaar after the vendor closed it up for the day, and slept there. I left before he came to open the stall each morning. But this morning I didn't wake up in time. He threatened to beat me if he sees me again."

"You're lucky he didn't guess that you're a girl," says Bibi Nusrat. The persimmon stops turning between Shaheed's fingers and the pink drains from his face and neck and he goes very still. He does not lift his eyes to meet Bibi Nusrat's. "What is your real name?" the teacher asks.

Shaheed hands the persimmon back to Bibi Nusrat and leans forward as if to bolt from the room. The child's eyes dart into every corner, as if looking for the windows, doors, any way out.

"You don't need to be afraid," Bibi Nusrat tells him. "You can stay here. You'll be safe."

"How did you know?" the girl-dressed-as-a-boy asks.

"For one thing, you look nothing like a boy," says Bibi Nusrat, standing and crossing to the window that looks out over the street. She peers up the street toward town and back down toward the bazaar, then draws the edges of the heavy velvet drapes tightly together and sits again. "For another, your hands are rough and red from scrubbing—scrubbing is girls' work."

The girl looks at the floor and the color returns to her face. She still looks as if she might jump up and run away.

"My name is Najmah," she says. "Najmah Marwari."

"Your name means 'star'," says Bibi Nusrat. "That's much better than 'martyr', which is what you'll become if you keep pretending you're a boy. It's a wonder anyone believed you at all."

"I had no choice," says the girl.

"Of course you didn't," says Bibi Nusrat. "Life is difficult enough for a girl, impossible for a girl without a family."

"I fooled enough people to get me here," says Najmah, "and I will fool enough to get me back." Her face takes on a sharp line at the jaw.

It's Bibi Nusrat's turn to be quiet. She crosses to turn on the electric lamps that stand in opposite corners of the room on slender pedestals. The light falls from beneath their fringed shades to leave dim little pools on the faded, dark red Turkoman carpet. When Bibi Nusrat sits again on the straight-backed chair across from Najmah she has made up her mind.

"You must stay here," she says, and Najmah leans back a little, as if it's the first time she's relaxed in a long while. "But you cannot go on pretending to be a boy. It isn't safe. You must be who you are and cover your head when you go out. I will take care of you. In return you can help Husna in the kitchen and study your numbers." Bibi Nusrat says this with finality, as if it's all settled.

"That's not possible," says Najmah, and her voice is strong, the set of her eyes hardening to match the line of her jaw. "I must return to my village. I must do as my father wished."

"If your father and brother are dead, what will be in the village for you?" asks Bibi Nusrat. "You weren't safe when your mother was alive—what chance will you have alone?" Najmah's gaze does not waver and she shakes her head. Bibi Nusrat leans back in her chair. Najmah appraises the teacher's blond hair and fair skin.

"You are not Muslim," Najmah says. "I do not expect you to understand."

"But I am Muslim," Bibi Nusrat says. "I became a Muslim when I married my husband in America. He came back to Afghanistan out of duty to his family and his country and I came with him. I understand very well." Bibi Nusrat is quiet for a moment. She met Faiz ul-Haq ten years ago when he was in medical school and she was a graduate student in New York. His deep sadness at being away from his country when his people were at war was what first drew her to him. She had never known anyone so committed to an ideal before—and it had never occurred to her that the place of one's birth might be an ideal to commit to until she met Faiz.

"Please think about it," Bibi Nusrat says. "If you stay, I'll help you find out what became of your father and your brother when the war is over." Najmah nods.

Bibi Nusrat sends Husna to the bazaar with enough rupees to buy Najmah a long skirt and tunic. She sits while Najmah eats vegetables and *naan* at the table. Najmah squirms uncomfortably on the chair and ignores the knife and fork beside her plate, eating with her right hand, mashing peas and potatoes together and sopping up gravy with pieces of *naan*. She slurps sweet green tea in over her teeth, and Bibi Nusrat smiles at the girl's good manners.

Afterward, Bibi Nusrat heats water for Najmah's bath. When Husna returns from the bazaar, she asks the servant to make up the extra bed for Najmah in the room across from her own, at the back of the bungalow, beside the kitchen.

Bibi Nusrat goes out to the garden while Najmah has her bath. She sets a kerosene lamp down on a small table under the persimmon tree and pulls the string cot from the kitchen stoop to an open spot between the tree and the garden wall. The rain has stopped and the sky is clear. The stars shimmer like diamonds stitched to a black velvet curtain. The rain has washed the stink of dust and diesel from the air, and acrid smoke from wood- and dung-fueled fires drifts from the refugee camps a few streets away.

Bibi Nusrat lies back on the cot and wraps her shawl tightly around her. The storm has brought chilled air from the mountains. She watches the stars rise and disperse, and wonders if Faiz is looking at them, too, whether he's safe and warm. He left for Kabul in April, long before tragedy struck in New York, to set up medical camps in the areas where the mujahideen fought the Taliban. He promised he'd return to Peshawar by the end of summer, but there had been no word from him since July. Bibi Nusrat looks up at the stars every night, and talks to them as if he can hear her words through them.

"I wish," she said, "I'd done what you wanted. I wish I'd conceived a child before you left. Perhaps you would have been more careful if you'd known you had a son to come home to." It always distresses her that she hears nothing back when she talks through the stars, but still it comforts her to send her words to Faiz through them.

Just then, a meteor arcs overhead, its tail a curving, silver streak behind it, and she hears behind her a sharp intake of breath. Bibi Nusrat sits up and turns to see Najmah standing in the golden light from the kerosene lamp, both hands clamped over her mouth, her eyes on the sky where the meteor disappears in a trail of silver.

"What is it?" Bibi Nusrat asks.

"Sword," Najmah whispers, her voice faint and shaking. "The sword is evil. Someone will die!" Bibi Nusrat stands and pulls the girl down on the cot beside her, and wraps her body-warmed shawl around them both.

"That wasn't a sword," Bibi Nusrat says, her voice a soothing murmur. "It was a meteor, a piece of rock broken from a comet hurtling through the sky." Najmah swings her head from side to side and her damp, long black hair whips the air like a horse's tail as she struggles free.

"There were hundreds of swords the night before my mother and brother died," she says. "Thousands, going in every direction all over the sky! When the sword appears in the sky, you know you'll draw your last allotted breath."

"No, Najmah," says Bibi Nusrat, turning so the lantern light falls on her face. "What you saw was a meteor storm—something that happens rarely. You're a shepherd—you've seen thousands of meteors cross the sky. It's a miracle of nature—not an omen of death!"

Two weeks earlier Bibi Nusrat had asked her husband's relatives to watch the Leonid meteor storm with her. Her sisters-and brothers-in-law and her neighbors also called the meteors "swords" and they stayed indoors, shut away from the bad omen. And so Bibi Nusrat had watched it with Fariel and her family who had come, Bibi Nusrat suspected, more for the food than the promise of shooting stars.

"The swords are myth," says Bibi Nusrat. "They're not real. Comets are ice and stone—they're real. Allah wanted comets and meteors to remind people that they should obey the Koran—and that's where the myth came from."

"They're evil," Najmah says again.

"Listen," says Bibi Nusrat. "In the holy city of Mecca is Islam's holiest place, in the center of which is the Ka'ba, which contains the black stone. You've heard of it."

Najmah nods. Every Muslim child knows about the Ka'ba and the holy black stone, and every Muslim must make a pilgrimage to the Ka'ba at least once in a lifetime.

"The black stone is a meteorite—it fell from the sky and landed on the earth and was brought to Mecca. How can it be evil if it's part of the world's holiest shrine?"

"Truly?" asks Najmah.

"Truly," Bibi Nusrat replies.

Najmah sits beside her on the cot. Bibi Nusrat wraps them both in the warm shawl again, and they watch the sky together. Bibi Nusrat points out constellations, which Najmah knows by other names, and Najmah points to the North Star.

"My father taught me to bring the sheep home safely through mountain pastures by making a fist and lining up the middle knuckle with the Star That Never Moves," says Najmah. "It's the most constant star, and I'm never lost knowing it's there."

How different Najmah's life would be in America, Bibi Nusrat thinks. With good nutrition and medical care and education, the possibilities for such an intelligent girl would be endless. The idea excites her and she lies awake thinking about it.

The next morning Bibi Nusrat takes a tray with bed tea to Najmah's room and knocks gently on the door. She waits a

moment before pushing the door open to find Najmah strug-
gling up from sleep to sit amid her tumbled sheets and quilt.
While Najmah rubs sleep from her eyes, Bibi Nusrat sets down
the tray, removes the cozy from the pot, and pours tea. The scent
of cardamom makes them both hungry.

"Will you come to class today?" asks Bibi Nusrat, sitting
beside her on the edge of the cot. Najmah's hair makes a silky
black curtain around her face and shoulders. Bibi Nusrat reaches
forward and tucks a loose strand behind the girl's ear. "Your
clothes are still drying in the garden, so you'll have to wear the
skirt. Your hair is too beautiful to stick under a turban." Najmah
smiles shyly and takes the teacup.

Bibi Nusrat lays out the tunic and skirt and a blue chador
of her own before collecting the tray and leaving Najmah to wash
and dress. After breakfast, Bibi Nusrat helps Husna prepare the
midday meal and drags the cots under the persimmon tree.

Fariel arrives first at Bibi Nusrat's back gate. She sits quietly
and waits for the others. Next Ahmed and Wali arrive in a bois-
terous knot with Farooq and Farid. When the children are
assembled on the cots under the persimmon tree, Bibi Nusrat
asks them to review what she's told them about division. She half
listens while she looks over their heads to the open kitchen door
to see whether Najmah will join them.

Beside the kitchen door Husna keeps a large curry bush
growing in a clay pot. Behind the shadowed movement of air
through oval leaves, Bibi Nusrat sees a tunic sleeve where
Najmah listens out of sight.

Just then, there is a disturbance at the garden gate, where
Haroon, the refugee camp *malek*, talks to a bearded stranger in an
extravagantly wound black turban.

"Ho!" Haroon calls out. Bibi Nusrat tells Farooq to continue, and crosses the garden to greet the two men. She talks over the gate without inviting them into the garden.

"This is Mohiuddin Marwari," says Haroon. "He is looking for his niece, an orphan from Kunduz." Bibi Nusrat feels as if a large piece of dry bread is stuck in her throat, and she swallows instead of answering. He wants to take this beautiful, bright girl back to Kunduz to marry off, she thinks. She'll have babies before her body is grown, and she'll die young in a mountain village.

"He thought perhaps, since children come here to your garden, the girl might have come ..." Haroon goes on. Bibi turns and looks over her shoulder at the children under the persimmon tree.

"Do you see her here?" she asks the man. A spot twitches between her shoulder blades and she prays that Najmah will stay hidden in the kitchen.

Beneath the broad-shouldered stranger's large turban sits a pair of humorless eyes that come to rest on Amina, Tahira, and Fariel. He grunts and turns toward Haroon, who studies the dirt in front of his sandals.

"Kunduz has been liberated," says Haroon. "The fighters are coming to take their families back to their villages. If you should see a tall, dark-haired girl of about twelve, please let me know."

"What does this man want with his niece?" Bibi Nusrat asks, trying not to sound as if she might not approve of the stranger's intentions. Haroon speaks in a low voice to the stranger and turns back to Bibi Nusrat.

"He wants to take her back to live in her village with his family," Haroon tells her. "He will claim his dead brother's property. She will live in the house where she grew up, *inshallah*."

"God willing," Bibi repeats softly. "If I see the girl I will tell you, Haroon." She nods toward the stranger and turns back to her students, who have abandoned their discussion of long division and are rolling about on the cots, laughing and tickling each other.

If the mujahideen are coming from Kunduz, Bibi Nusrat thinks, perhaps Faiz will come too! She takes Najmah's staying in the kitchen as a sign the girl doesn't want to go with her uncle.

In the jostling, the easel and chalkboard have fallen to the ground, and also the tray with the metal water tumblers. The children help her pick things up, and when they're seated again, Bibi Nusrat looks up to see Najmah sitting between Amina and Fariel on the girls' cot. The boys stare at her uncertainly, quiet for once.

"This is Najmah," says Bibi Nusrat, placing a hand on Najmah's shoulder. Najmah stares at her feet, encased in the too-large sandals of her older brother. "You saw her yesterday dressed as a boy."

"Why was she . . ." Wali begins to ask, but Ahmed pokes him with an elbow to silence him.

To distract them, Bibi Nusrat tells them to wash their hands for dinner. She sends Najmah to help Husna carry out trays, which contain salt-roasted chicken and *naan*.

After they have eaten, the children play in the garden, running and climbing on the blue-painted gate. When Bibi Nusrat calls them back to the cots under the persimmon tree, Najmah takes her place again.

That evening, as they eat leftover chicken and *naan* in the kitchen, Bibi Nusrat says, "Why didn't you come out to greet your uncle this afternoon?"

"He and my father were the only sons in their family,"

Najmah says. "They never got along. I don't want to live with him and his family."

"Do you want to go back to Kunduz?" Bibi Nusrat asks. "It's only a matter of time until Haroon learns you're here." Najmah doesn't answer.

In the following days news of Taliban defeats floods Peshawar, as more warriors come to take their families back to their villages in the North and to Kabul, even to Kandahar and other places liberated from Taliban rule. Tahira and Amina are the first students to leave, followed in the same week by Ahmed and Wali. Only Fariel, Najmah, Farooq, and Farid remain.

Najmah proves to be a quick student. She asks Bibi Nusrat to teach her English. They sit in the living room every day after the others leave and go over vocabulary. In a very short time, Bibi Nusrat and Najmah speak to each other in English.

Bibi Nusrat doesn't allow Najmah to go to the bazaar. She cautions Husna to tell no one that the girl stays with them. Even in the garden, Najmah must cover her head. Two weeks later, Mohiuddin Marwari still has not returned to look for Najmah, and Bibi Nusrat begins to wonder whether she only imagined his visit. But when she feels anxiety grasping at her heart, she knows Mohiuddin is real—not a sword in the sky, but ice and rock, like a meteor.

It's nearly Christmas when the new rulers take their seats in Kabul, and still there is no word from Faiz. The fighting has stopped in Kunduz. Bibi Nusrat writes notes to send with any mujahideen who is going back inside Afghanistan. Some are going to Kandahar and Tora Bora to fight. Since she doesn't know where Faiz is, she sends a note with anyone who will carry it, marked "To Dr. Faiz ul-Haq, Surgeon."

One evening, when Najmah is in her room studying her list of English words, and Husna has gone to her room behind the kitchen for the night, there is a knock at the front door. Bibi Nusrat sits in the worn armchair writing a letter to her mother. Her heart leaps at the rapping, and she thinks that, finally, someone has come to bring her news of Faiz. But when she swings open the front door, Haroon and Mohiuddin stand on her front steps.

"*A-salaam-alei-kum!*" says Haroon curtly. "Someone told Mr. Mohiuddin they saw his niece Najmah come to your house." Mohiuddin stands mute and sullen beside him.

"A girl did come looking for work," she replies, again not inviting them in. "But I already have a servant. The girl said her family lives in the city, not in the camps. I sent her to Dr. Munir's house. Why don't you check there?" Although it's true that she sent a girl to work for Dr. Munir, Bibi Nusrat knows it will buy her only a little time.

Mohiuddin looks past Bibi Nusrat, into the house. She allows enough time for him to see the living room is empty before saying good night and shutting the door. She leans against it and doesn't dare to breathe. She feels her heart hammer inside her throat. The two men talk quietly on the other side of the door, but she can't hear their words. After a few minutes she hears their feet on the steps. She waits for the groan of the gate, and does not hear it.

Bibi Nusrat tiptoes down the hallway to Najmah's door at the back of the house, and lets herself in without knocking. Najmah looks up from her vocabulary list in surprise. Bibi Nusrat puts her finger to her lips and switches off the light. She crosses to Najmah's cot and sits.

"Your uncle was here," she whispers against the girl's ear. "They may be listening in the garden." She places a finger against Najmah's lips and feels the girl's breath against her knuckle. She rises and the cot strings squeak loudly against their wooden frame. Bibi Nusrat goes to the window. Although she sees no one in the garden, she returns to whisper to Najmah that she must go to sleep and not turn the light on again.

Bibi Nusrat goes to her own room and lies in the dark, still dressed. She stares up at the ceiling, where she has pasted small iridescent plastic stars. A tear trickles from the corner of her eye and falls into her ear. She wipes angrily at her face. Where is Faiz? How could he leave her in this place, where men like Mohiuddin Marwari come to menace her? Her heart hurts and another tear pools in the small well between her eye and nose.

She repeats what she always tells herself to calm her fears: that Faiz is busy treating the injured; he won't return until the war is completely finished; he'll be the last to come home. Still, in the morning, when the garden gate creaks beside the persimmon tree, she awakens with her heart leaping. Then she remembers it's the farmer who brings fresh milk to Husna in the kitchen each morning. To keep herself from thinking of Faiz she rises to take Najmah her bed tea.

A letter comes from Bibi Nusrat's mother in New York, addressed to Elaine Perrin Faiz. In the letter, her mother begs her to come home. "Your place is here," her mother writes. "You can't wait for Faiz forever. Without him there is nothing for you in Peshawar." Her mother's words sting her whenever she thinks of them during the day.

That evening, Bibi Nusrat lies on the cot in the garden, wrapped in her shawl against the cold, and looks up at the stars.

"I won't leave here, Faiz, until I know what's happened to you," she begins. "If you don't come back, I'll take Najmah with me. She'll be our daughter." It shocks her a little to realize she has just imagined a life without Faiz.

Najmah comes out to keep watch beside her.

"Who were you talking to?" Najmah asks.

"My husband," says Bibi Nusrat.

"Does he answer?"

"No," she replies. They lie quietly under their shawls for a while, and a comet streaks into view, leaving a long silver stream in its wake.

"Look!" says Najmah in English. "A meteorite!" Bibi Nusrat hugs the girl.

"You've learned so much in a short time, Najmah," says Bibi Nusrat. "I've been thinking . . ." Najmah looks up at her. "Perhaps Faiz will not come back from this war."

"You mustn't say that!" says Najmah. "He'll come—you'll see!"

"What I've been thinking," says Bibi Nusrat, "is that I will go back to America, to teach in New York. You could come with me and go to the International School. Would you like that?"

"Can you see the stars in New York?" Najmah asks after a moment's silence.

"Yes," says Bibi Nusrat, "of course you can see the stars. Because of the city lights they're dimmer than they are here, but there are many other things to see in New York." Suddenly the idea excites her. I can do this, she thinks.

"But you cannot see the mountains," says Najmah.

"In New York there are buildings as tall as mountains," Bibi Nusrat says, and thinks of New York's twin towers, which were as tall as mountains, but are no more.

"My entire life I have lived in the shadow of the Hindu Kush," says Najmah. "My heart would cry if I could not see the mountains every day."

"But Najmah," says Bibi Nusrat, "you would have so many other things—school, friends, family. You will have enough to eat and good care and a good education. If you stay here, your life will be very difficult."

"You've given me stories about the stars," Najmah says quietly. "I will have them forever. I won't know where I am if I cannot see the North Star."

Bibi Nusrat holds the girl close to her. She thinks of the value of the life of a girl named "Star" living in a village of Afghanistan. It is much greater than the value of the life of a woman with no husband in Pakistan. She and Najmah count four more meteorites through the bare branches of the persimmon tree before they go inside, and Bibi Nusrat thinks of stone and ice—so cold to give such fierce light.

REACTING AND RECOVERING

"It is a dangerous world but it is wonderful, too . . ."

REACTING AND
RECOVERING

Even for professional and often published authors, finding the right ways and words to react to 9/11 was a challenge. Marion Dane Bauer calls it "the most difficult thing I have ever faced." Her struggle led her to write both a personal essay and a poem. Jaime and Arnold Adoff also responded with poems, concrete poems whose construction on the page evokes the wreckage and the raw emotions that twist across our memories of 9/11. Walter Dean Myers writes a letter from London that is a harrowing indictment of violence, which makes enemies of strangers and destroys hope for dialogue that might otherwise foster recovery. On 9/11, Naomi Shihab Nye was with students in Oklahoma, a state that is no stranger to the horrors of terrorism. She recalls how words, then and since, help shape our experience of things, even disastrous things, providing a kind of supportive chair in which we can sit and reflect. In a poem, Sharon Creech reacts to 9/11 by turning our thoughts to the survivors and their desire for the return of those who were lost. Betsy Hearne also writes of survival and return by celebrating the power of stories, which she compares with the mythical phoenix that is reborn from its own ashes—ashes similar, perhaps, to those left by the destruction of 9/11. And, finally, there is a personal essay from New Zealand author Margaret Mahy. Just as Katherine Paterson's essay—the first to arrive—was the perfect way to begin this book of help, hope, and healing, so Margaret Mahy's—the last to arrive—is the perfect way to conclude it. For it returns the events of that day to a global perspective; it reminds us how very connected we all are to one another in this ever-smaller world; it grapples, too, with the interconnectedness—and occasional disjunctions—of story and truth, of imagination and reality. And it reminds us that, yes, "it is a dangerous world but it is wonderful, too."

A WHITE AMERICAN'S LAMENT

BY MARION DANE BAUER

We crossed the ocean seeking opportunity,
seeking freedom,
seeking peace.
Surely it wasn't our fault
that we found our opportunity occupied
by those we named Indians,
though they had never seen India;
redskins,
though their skins were not red,
savages,
though it was we who taught them
the subtle art of scalping.

What could we do but fill
their empty bellies with promises?
And when men and women,
children, too,
innocent—
were we not innocent?—
fell before their swift retribution,
we were afraid.
So we put a bounty on savage red Indian scalps—
the Christian ones were the easiest to obtain;
they had learned to trust us—
and spent the next centuries slaughtering
and confining
and oppressing
and civilizing.
How many more centuries must we spend
trying to understand
trying to atone?
We were afraid,
and remember,
we crossed the ocean seeking peace.

We do not believe in hate.
But when those black hands tending our crops
and our babies
were set free, at last,
we were afraid.
Might they not
attack our daughters, our sisters, our mothers
in their chaste beds?

And so we hooded our faces
behind more white
and left our mark—
KKK—
on their bodies,
on their souls.
Remember, though,
we were afraid.
And we do not believe in hate.

We welcome all to our shores.
This melting pot.
This new, better way.
But when they dropped the bombs on Pearl Harbor
we were afraid.
And so we gathered all who looked like them,
who spoke like them,
who surely believed like them
behind barbed wire,
because we knew they would bomb us next.
We must protect our children.
We will deal with the regrets later,
and perhaps even one day
we will, once more,
when we are not afraid,
welcome all to our shores.

A plane crashes into a tower.
Two planes.
Two towers.
Another into the heart
of our ability to make war.
We are afraid.
We are afraid.
We are afraid.
What will they do next?
What will we do?
A plane crashes into a tower.

TWO SMALL IDEAS

The date was September 10, 2001, an ordinary day in Minnesota. Blue with the first hints of fall in the air. I'd been for my usual long morning walk with my sheltie, Mr. Spriggan, and had settled in to eat my breakfast and read the newspaper. My gaze fell on a headline. Something about the peace talks in the Middle East coming to nothing again. I turned the page without reading farther. I'd had enough. I didn't want to know anything more about the failing peace in the Middle East. Yet, even as I turned the page, I found myself wondering. How much longer would it be before we weren't just reading about the chaos in the Middle East but finding ourselves embroiled in it?

How much longer turned out to be twenty-four hours. Exactly.

I am not a particularly political person. I keep myself well enough informed to be able to vote with reasonable assurance in local and national elections and consider doing so both a responsibility and a privilege. What I mean, though, by not being political, is that I tend neither to work for nor to expect large answers to large problems. And I am always enormously glad not to be in a position to have to make the decisions national and global problems require of our leaders. I'll just stay home and write another children's book, thank you very much.

As the world spins out of control around me, I've just finished writing a historical novel set on the Minnesota prairie in the late nineteenth century and another about a wolf pup. I've also completed a counting/colors picture book called *One Brown Bunny.* I am presuming, whatever else happens, we will go on teaching our children their numbers and their colors. In other words, I have returned to business as usual, as our leaders have requested.

Consistently, however, in the days that have followed the tragedy in New York and Washington, D.C., and Pennsylvania, I have had two thoughts, entirely unrelated to one another, both related to the uncertain days we now face. One is of the Minnesota Dakota War, which occurred in 1862.

The Minnesota Dakota War came about for an accumulation of complex reasons—as is usual with wars. The Dakota people had been confined to a prairie reservation and forbidden their accustomed hunting grounds. Cultural and religious changes were being forced upon them. Dakota warriors were punished if they made even the smallest forays against the Ojibway, their traditional enemy, despite the fact that the rest of the United States was engaged in a civil war. And the government had made and then broken promise after promise, resulting in humiliation and starvation for the Dakota people.

Bitter resentment turned deadly when four Dakota hunters had an angry altercation with some settlers and killed them. The tribe was left with a choice: turn the men over to the white authorities or go to war with them. The majority of the tribe did not want to go to war. Those who did joined together and virtually depopulated twenty-three southwestern Minnesota counties. In six weeks of fighting nearly five hundred whites, most of them civilians, and an unknown but significant number of Dakota were killed. When peace was restored, four hundred full- or mixed-blood Dakota were brought before a military tribunal, and 303 were sentenced to hang. Only President Lincoln's intervention—many of the trial transcripts were found to be filled with errors—brought the number actually hanged down to thirty-nine.

Why am I thinking of such a long-ago incident as we face our crisis in the year 2001? Because I have just been working with the stories of settlers who moved to Minnesota only eleven years after that war and thus have had to face the reality of the terror many of them must have still felt, given the recent reality of that event. It is common today to talk about—if not to actually try to do anything about—the injustice done to the native people whose land we whites "discovered." So common that we forget the fear most of those settlers lived with every day of their lives. And perhaps we forget, too, that fear is the first breeding ground for hate.

I know pacifists who are, nonetheless, behind today's war against the terrorists. I have no criticism for their change of heart. As we face the uncertainty that now taints air travel, working in tall buildings, even opening our mail and breathing our air—and who knows what else tomorrow?—I will readily admit I have no better solution than the war our leaders have proclaimed. I, too, have long called myself a pacifist, though I have always been aware that pacifism is an easy stance to take when wars happen *over there*. When my own person, my own family and friends, are under threat, turning the other cheek doesn't seem quite so easy. When I am afraid—when we are all afraid—loving the enemy becomes very difficult indeed.

It is so curiously like this country that I love, in all of its bumblings through the world, to be dropping food and bombs at the same time. I have been heartened by the simple goodwill behind such an unlikely idea. I have been amused, too, in a knowing way, to read that the food bundles include an American staple, peanut butter and jelly, something few in Afghanistan have ever seen before, something I suspect few have ever wished would come plummeting from their sky. We do have a way of assuming that our tastes are, of course, the tastes of all the world.

Nonetheless, I rejoice in our generosity. At least, dropping food to starving people is not an act of fear. And I can only hope that when the fear is past, we will be more generous still. The real basis for the fierce resentment toward our country from this part of the world lies in the deep poverty of so many, many people. A Middle Eastern Marshall Plan, such as we created to help war-ravaged Europe after World War II, could change the face of our world in ways bombs never will. Only by following such a concerted effort to improve others' lives might we have good reason to put aside our fear.

But I said at the beginning I have had two thoughts in response to this crisis. One, I am fearfully aware of what fear does to us all. The way it diminishes our humanity. The way it seeks to place blame. The other is a simple mistrust of large solutions to large problems.

I know. Of course. Large problems demand large solutions, and sometimes thinking big can actually transform the world. A case in point is the Marshall Plan I just mentioned. Or to take another example from the same time, the GI Bill, following World War II, sent thousands upon thousands of young men to college who never would have had a chance for education beyond high school. GI loans made it possible, too, for the first time, for great numbers of ordinary families to own their own homes. Those two acts together created our present middle class.

But despite occasional big answers that work, I remain skeptical. So much harm can come hidden in good intentions. Subsidized housing for the poor tore down neighborhoods where people cared about people and created high-rise concrete sewers where crime is in control. Even the development of the spectacular and oh-so-efficient skyscraper is what made this recent atrocity possible.

My answer? I'm not certain it is a completely ethical one, but it has been mine for many years. I said in the beginning that I am not a political person. I don't join demonstrations to try to alter government policies, even when I disagree with those policies. I seldom even join organizations formed to bring about needed change. I do what good I am going to do in the world very simply, very quietly, and entirely one-on-one.

My contribution to foreign relations has been, several times, to have a foreign exchange student as part of my family. My concern for needy children has prompted me to be a foster parent. I have one talent. I can write for kids. And so I make myself available to other writers who want to do what I do. I figure this way, one-on-one, the good I can do is limited, but the harm is limited, too.

My answer is too small. I know. And the problems that face us are large. And yet if everyone tried it . . .

Two small ideas. Two small ideas in the face of an enormous crisis. One, beware of fear. Decisions made in fear can damage our humanity for years to come. Two, we can change the world, you and I. We can and are changing the world, one by one by one by one . . .

NOT LIKE TV

BY JAIME ADOFF

Talking on my cell phone, on my way for the first time.
People say, it's not like what you see
on
tv . . .
Watching from the safety of—not like what you see
on
tv
watching from your couch. The screen softens the blow.
(You can always change the channel, you know.)
Anger starts to boil up as I think about
what
they
did

to my city—to our country.

What

they

did.

People just going to work, a normal kiss goodbye, never expecting to die.

As I turn the corner I'm in midsentence when I get to Park Place, not just a name on a game board, this place is real—close, too close . . .

I try to find words, to finish my sentence but they've all run away.

All my words—running back towards West Broadway,

running fast uptown. Taking the same path as those lucky ones, who were able to run.

As I turn the corner, reality smacks me in the face and kicks me in the stomach.

It's not like what you see

on

tv . . .

That last piece of twisted metal hovering over what once was.

Looking like the grim reaper, five stories high.

People come and go, paying respects—cameras flash.

The gate opens and I see them, single file:

Staggering out of the rubble—blank-faced, dust-covered—stunned disbelief screaming

in their eyes. Like an old movie reel of mine workers after a collapse,

happy to be alive,

but

not really
happy.
They carry untold souls on their shoulders, buckets of
agony in twelve-hour shifts.
Digging through hell, I can tell, they've seen things a person
should never have to see.
Seen things they'll want to forget, but never will.
Their dreams must be worse than any horror movie ever
made.
My thoughts drift away on smoke and ash
as the last recovery worker passes by . . .
His hard hat twisted, like it's *trying* to slide off his head.
One side of overalls falls down to very wide waist.
Everything on his body—trying to run away. Trying to escape.
He looks through me, through the small crowd.
Walking past a newswoman interviewing a cop, he doesn't stop.
I turn my head and he's gone. Gone into the dust.
You can feel the loss of life pouring through the gate, you
can feel . . .
all the husbands and wives and sons and daughters and fathers
and mothers and brothers and sisters . . .
I'm taking it all in, trying to at least.
It's too much. All the suffering starts to seep into my pores, filling me with despair and
pain, and hate—but there's a moment. A second where I think I
can feel what *they* felt,
what they felt in that instant the sky fell, and the ground caved
in below them.
For a second, I think I can *feel*
What they felt . . .

For a second
I think I can.
For a second.

It's not like what you see
on
tv

not like that at all . . .

LEIGH CALLS FROM BERLIN: SHE SHOUTS TURN ON SEEENEN

BY ARNOLD ADOFF

just as the first taste of coffee in the Ohio morning
just as the second plane i n t o the secondbuilding
just as the collapse of concrete and steel and sanity
just as the poet's steel of peace and self-deception
             blows up Broadway and across the HudsonRiver
             and rains sweet souls forever onto this roof.

M a   r   t   i   n
M a   r   t   i   n
   h   e   l   p
       m y
  s   w   e   e   t
m   e   m   o   r   y:
  s   t   e   e   l
m   e   m   o   r   y   of Memphis a l m o s t long ago motel
          and somewhere in the simple bushes away
          from cameras a single rifle steel shines.

I am writing   this on the celebration of your birthday.
I am writing this onto a celebration of your birthday,
                                   my
steel keys explodingletters into sense in the old way
of working onto a structure: words *try* the definition
of s e n s e.   Alchemy: image into worth into thought.

There is a long history here, this old blood into new.
I study andremember all the broken bodies: souls rise
without reason long before their reasonable   t i m e s.

Martin, I cannot t u r n a New Testament c h e e k.

    I can onlyhope tokeep myfists in emptypockets.

ENEMIES

BY WALTER DEAN MYERS

Most of the year I live in New Jersey, but for six weeks each year I live abroad. The neighborhood in which I rent a one-bedroom flat each fall is located off Edgeware Road in London. Edgeware Road branches out from Marble Arch and the busy stores of Oxford Street. The area is home for London's relatively large Middle Eastern community. I've always felt comfortable in the section that one Londoner described as the "Bayswater Arab Emirate." I became accustomed to the veiled women and men in robes. When the men spoke to me on the streets in Arabic, I would apologize and explain that I did not speak the language.

For the last ten years I have felt comfortable. This year was different. This was the year of the attacks on the World Trade Center, the year of horrible images filling my television screen.

The Middle Eastern men are, in the main, not doing well in London. They are the ones who clean the streets, who wash dishes in restaurants, who haul away trash. Often they don't have jobs and mill around in the evenings in the coffee shops along Edgeware. I am reminded of the young black men on street corners in Harlem and Bedford Stuyvesant in Brooklyn.

While the general reaction of the British public to the September attacks on America was, predictably, outrage and anger, the reaction of at least some of the young men on Edgeware Road was different. They were not offended by the attacks, conducted in the name of their religion, but actually proud.

Each time the *London Times* reported bombings in Afghanistan, young men with beards would respond by setting off powerful fireworks along Edgeware Road. The shoppers, white, Indian, African, Middle Easterners, coming from the Safeway supermarket would walk a little faster, clutch their bags a little tighter, and breathe a little shallower in recognition that these were troubled times. The young men setting off the fireworks, some in their late teens, others appearing somewhat older, swaggered and laughed. This was their time. They were the impotent grown potent, the unimportant now on the covers of the world's journals.

The most telling moment was on the day a plane came down in Queens, an event that does not seem to be connected with terrorism. I watched as a group of young men stood in front of an appliance store and watched the events on a television in the window. They were cheering the destruction of the plane, apparently hoping that it was caused by someone spouting Islamic slogans. I watched one young man in particular: he was slapping the backs of his fellow watchers and making a big show of his glee at the image of the burning plane, of the death of Americans. Yes, we were enemies.

My mind went to another young man. It's never far from my sons, especially when either of them is in harm's way. On the twelfth of September my eldest son, Michael, was told to pack his bags and be ready to leave his California home within a half hour. Within a week he was headed toward the Middle East. Michael's a Protestant chaplain in the air force, and he's already served in combat zones in Eastern Europe, as well as South America.

And so there are these two young men, Michael, and the young man gloating over the burning plane. They are enemies. They are approximately the same coloring, and the same age. They both profess beliefs in a loving, merciful God. There will be no discussions, no heated arguments between them, no dialogue beyond the dismal correspondence of mass violence. I know that the young man on Edgeware Road has been failed by the economy of whatever Islamic country he claims as home. He has been left with a system of life that bars him from much of the modern world, and a state of poverty he despises. There is little sophistication in his thinking as he blames America for the condition that far too many Islamic people face, even in relatively well off countries such as Egypt and Malaysia. But, as he stands in front of that shop window, cheering the death of Americans, his lack of sophistication doesn't matter. He is my enemy because those who think like he does have brought their violence and hatred to my door, and to the doors of those I love. When, a few days later, an Iranian driver tells me that America must understand the needs of Islamic people for peace and justice, I am deaf. The murders have nothing to do with the remote rationalization of Islam, or of my son's Protestant ministry. They are the arguments of rapists talking about a need for love, and looters babbling about social protest.

On the Sunday before we leave, my wife and I go to see a movie, *Kandahar*. On the way, we are briefly caught up in an antiwar demonstration. The Socialist Party has made up signs, and young whites and Middle Easterners march through the streets of London to Trafalgar Square. The movie, made several years ago, is heavy-handed in spots but still frightening. It shows a part of the world where life is a constant struggle for survival, and where hope is trampled in the name of religious idealism. It is easy to understand how young men can be seduced to violence by anyone offering a taste of power.

But, at the end of the day, the man I don't know on Edgeware Road is still my enemy. When evil is loosed upon the world, all humanity becomes vulnerable. We choose sides and hope that the one we choose has some resemblance to the morality we espouse. I suspect it is a human, not merely personal, failure that his imperfect reasons for wanting to kill me are matched by my imperfect reasons for wanting to kill him. As I pass him on the streets of London, I think that he is satisfied that I will not find sleep easy that night, and he is right. But when I do sleep I will dream of killing my enemies.

WORDS TO SIT IN,
LIKE CHAIRS

BY NAOMI SHIHAB NYE

I was with teenagers at the wonderful Holland Hall School in
Tulsa when the planes flew into the buildings on September 11,
2001. We were talking about words as ways to imagine one
another's experience. A boy had just thanked me for a poem
about Jerusalem that enabled him to consider the Palestinian
side of the story. He said he had never thought about that perspective before, so the poem was important to him.

The TV commentators were already saying the hijackers
had been Arabs, which sent a deep chill into my Arab-American
blood. I said to those beautiful students, "Please, I beg you, if
Arabs are involved in this tragedy, remember there are millions
of Arabs who would never do such a thing."

They nodded soberly. "Of course," they said. "We know
that. This is Oklahoma." Their kindness overwhelmed me.

Then a boy said, "I hate to ask this so soon after it happened, but do you think you will write about it?"

"It would not be my choice of topic," I said, feeling sick, my head spinning, "but as writers, we are always exploring what happens, what comes next, turning it over, finding words to sit in like chairs, even in terrible scenery, so maybe I will have to write about it; maybe we all will. Because words shape the things that we live, whether beautiful or sorrowful, and help us connect to one another, this will be part of our history now."

Then a boy gave me a "Collapse-It" laundry basket that his parents had invented. Made of some kind of modern, waterproof, heavy-duty cardboard, it folded flat when not in use. He seemed mournful, handing it over.

"I brought this for you as a small gift," he said, "but after what happened today, it almost seems inappropriate."

Collapse-It. All Fall Down.

I clutched it to my chest and carried it with me on the long bus ride (since the planes were not flying) home to south Texas.

I have used the neat little white basket every time I've washed clothes since then. What came to me on a day of horror and tragedy and terrible mess, accompanied by kind words, continues as a helpful friend in daily life. Just the way words help us all not to be frozen in horror and fear.

USE WORDS. It is the most helpful thing I have learned in my life. We find words, we select and arrange them, to help shape our experiences of things. Whether we write them down for ourselves or send them into the air as connective lifelines between us, they help us live, and breathe, and see.

When I felt the worst after September 11, I called people. How is it for you? What are you thinking about? Have you heard anything helpful lately? Many of you probably did that, too. Sometimes it seemed good, and important, to call unexpected people—people who were not, in any way, expecting to hear from us right then. Hello, I'm thinking of you. Do you have any good news? If I had heard a useful quote or story recently myself, I shared it. Talking with friends felt like a connected chain. We passed things on down the wire.

It was very helpful for me to talk with Arab-American friends who automatically shared the doubled sense of sorrow. A poet friend of mine in New York City, just blocks from the disaster, said his wife saw him staring at a wall in their apartment one day, and said, "Don't withdraw! Speak!"

Sometimes we have to remind one another.

I also wrote sentences and phrases down in small notebooks, as I have done almost every day of my life since I was six. It is the best clue I know for how to stay balanced as we live. Bits and pieces of lines started fitting together again, offering small scraps of sense, ways out of the turmoil-of-mind, shining as miniature beacons, from under heaps of leaves.

Very rarely did I hang up from speaking with anyone or close my notebook feeling worse. Usually, that simple sharing of feelings, whether with another person, or with a patient page, helped ease the enormous feeling that the sorrow was too big to get one's mind around.

War is too big to get one's mind around too.

I keep thinking—if people who are angry, or frustrated, could use words instead of violence, how would our world be different? Maybe if enough of us keep in practice using our own honest words, that basic human act can help balance bigger things in the world.

THE SURVIVORS

BY SHARON CREECH

All they want
is the return
of husbands and wives
sisters and brothers
children
colleagues
friends.

That is all.

It is so little
and so much.

We can help them

recover and regain,
restore and resume.

We can comfort
their spouses,
their children,
their sisters and brothers,
their parents and grandparents,
colleagues and friends.

We can share their
sorrow
loss
burden.

We can remember.

It is so little
and so much.

SURVIVAL BY STORY

BY BETSY HEARNE

The phoenix is a bird that dies in fire every five hundred years. Yet always, from its ashes, arises a newborn bird. This mythical creature has survived in human lore since ancient times and has flown across continents of imagination for a reason: because all of us know that some stories have no happy ending—at times, we must somehow simply start over. The unearthly crimson-and-gold phoenix has risen recently in my own mind, engraved as it is since September 11 with the image of an unearthly crimson-and-gold explosion that held no happy endings for those immolated, for those left behind to grieve, or for those—especially the young—shaken by the sudden possibilities of random, heartless death. We can never recover the perished or the perishable sense of security that died on that day. We must start over with what rises from the ashes. But how? "September 11 was the end of my childhood," said one young New Yorker as she told the stories of her experience that day.

It is those stories that have survived the end of her childhood. It is stories that survive us. Our stories begin before birth and extend beyond death into the memory of those affected by our briefly flickering, fragile lives. Stories, which seem so ephemeral, often last longer than physical realities. As one of Isaac Bashevis Singer's characters says, "Today we live, but by tomorrow today will be a story. The whole world, all human life, is one long story."

We humans are a narrative species. In the concentration camp, starving inmates stuffed bits and pieces of their story into stone walls. In a sunken Russian submarine, the dying sailor used his last breath to write what was happening. The true dimensions of the events we have mourned since September 11 emerge in stories of life, death, and response. As listeners, we build complete stories out of fragments, for stories are what is heard, interpreted, and imagined, as well as what is told, and every story is a collaboration of teller and listener or reader. Phone messages from the doomed become capsules of a life imagined by us, or retold by the caller's loved ones in person, in print, and in electronic media.

Beyond such tragedies the pathway to recovery often lies through stories of humor or chance or apparent diversion that allow symbolic encounter and restoration. In 1945, Jean Cocteau shocked a French population devastated by World War II with his filming of "Beauty and the Beast," a fairy tale that seemed of slight importance compared to the harsh realities of survival. Yet Cocteau was dealing with survival—even revival—of the spirit. He saw his work as archeology of the soul, as resurrection and redemption of the human spirit from the ruins of the war. In that same period, a Jewish refugee named Jella Lepman returned to Germany, where she founded the International Youth Library—and later the International Board on Books for Young People—amidst the ruins of Munich, because she believed that the real hope for peace lay in crossing boundaries with books instead of bombs, in children's understanding their common humanity through reading stories about one another. Today, the stories emerging from our recent devastation have already drawn us closer across many boundaries. Ultimately, one of those boundaries we cross, over the story bridge of our common humanity, must be one that separates us from our enemies. The phoenix, according to Greek legend, lived in Arabia but flew everywhere—and reached, eventually, the life-giving sun.

COLLIDING STORIES

BY MARGARET MAHY

The phone rang in the early hours of the morning. Well, I am used
to that. I am a writer, living in New Zealand, and my publishers
(being largely on the other side of the world) are in a different
time zone. Anyhow, as I reached for the phone I was aware that,
once again, I had gone to sleep while blinking at the ancient television that stands at the foot of my bed. I often go to sleep,
entranced by the late-night news, which can be rather like watching
a series of quick horror stories.

That television set was speaking to me in a voice both
urgent and serious. The voice at the other end of the phone—a
voice that belonged to my daughter in London—was urgent and
serious, too.

"Something terrible has happened," she told me.
"Terrorists have attacked New York. They have crashed planes
into the World Trade Center."

As she spoke, I found myself focusing on the colored image of a plane flying toward a tall, vaguely familiar building then seeming to vanish into it. For half a second it looked as if the building had somehow absorbed the plane . . . as if all might yet be well. Then a wounding explosion burst out on the side of the building.

The world is full of atrocity. In spite of attempts to build better and happier societies, people are constantly doing terrible things to one another. All the same, this attack seemed particularly shocking, partly because it was more personal than most. New York City had always seemed not only amazing, but invulnerable to any attack. Yet someone had struck out at it, and friends of mine might be among the dead or injured. As I sat there, blinking at the old television set at two o'clock in the New Zealand morning, watching New York while listening to my daughter's voice from London, London and New York (the world's greatest cities) melted into Governors Bay (a small straggling village on the edge of Lyttelton Harbour in the South Island of New Zealand). The world remade itself.

Suddenly it was brought home to me—and probably to everyone watching these terrible events—that there was no such thing as true safety. My daughter and I said goodbye to one another, but I went on listening and staring. Over and over again, on that small oblong screen at the foot of my bed, the great building exploded . . . and exploded . . . and exploded. And then, perhaps most horrific of all, we were shown images of Islamic children—all boys—laughing and cheering, applauding what was apparently (to them at least) a victory. It was as if I was watching the collision not only of planes and buildings but of two opposing stories. I was in New Zealand, and they were in Pakistan. We were watching the same picture and hearing the same news. But I was receiving a very different story from the story that was affecting those dancing, cheering boys.

All that night and over the next two days, New Zealand television abandoned its usual programs and played ongoing accounts of the attack on the World Trade Center. I was to see, over and over again, that plane flying into the tower, that instant of hesitation, and then that devastating explosion. And over and over again, commentators incredulously declared that it was like watching some special effect in a film. Once upon a time, in the very early days of film, people screamed and shrank back in their seats as black-and-white trains came rushing out of the screen toward them. But films and television are so much part of our lives by now that things were the other way round for us—it was hard for us to believe that what we were being shown was real. Once the image had seemed like reality. Now reality seemed like the image. That moment of impact still looks to me like some clever trick. But, of course, it is not. Hundreds of people died in that moment. And men from another land were prepared to kill themselves in order to achieve this savage crisis. In some parts of the world those men are heroes. It is hard to make sense of it all.

Many people in New Zealand feel they belong with the USA. This is not only because we speak the same language, but because, for many years, New Zealanders have been thrilled by the stories and films that flow out of the USA, and have danced to its music, too. Of course we do make our own films; we have our own music. All the same, the sounds that have dominated our radio programs and the images that fill our screens are largely American. As nations, we live by approximately similar rules, laugh at the same jokes, and weep over the same tragedies. I was a child during the Second World War. I remember vividly just how American intervention in the Pacific protected New Zealand from possible Japanese invasion. I remember just how glamorous American servicemen seemed to be and how welcome they were when they were on leave in our cities and towns. Of course, these days New Zealand and the USA live different political lives and, though they agree about many fundamental things, they can disagree, too. Yet, deep down, the old connections and sympathies are still there. And these days there are many more family ties than there used to be. Back in the 1940s, some New Zealand girls married some of those visiting servicemen and went back to the USA with them. Families have come from the USA to make their homes in New Zealand. My son-in-law, who lives five minutes down the road from me, was born in Vermont. His Quaker parents came to New Zealand at the time of the Cuban missile crisis, and in an odd way, I regard Vermont as *my* own home state, simply because my son-in-law (a true New Zealander by now) was born there. My own books were first published in the USA. Watching the World Trade Center buildings fall, I remembered the first time, when, visiting New York, I had had those two towers pointed out to me. New Zealand and the USA are on different sides of the world, but we are connected by history, by family and friendship, and by stories, too.

Stories! I am a writer of stories for children and young adults. Some of the books I write are very simple ones and some are complicated, but nearly all of them have real events worked into them—real events that are somehow linked with fantasy and folktale. I am used to editing these stories. I cut out pieces—sometimes true pieces—because they feel as if they are clogging the main action. I make some characters heroes and I make others villains by simplifying them . . . by emphasizing certain actions and ideas, and by trimming others away. I think— indeed, I *know*—that stories are powerful in human life. When I was a child, there were certain tales I loved so deeply (Kipling's tale *The Jungle Book* was one of them) that I tried to drag them into my everyday life and live them myself. On that morning in September, as I watched the World Trade Center buildings fall, I felt I must be living through part of an invented story, and I know many other people felt the same. As I watched those Pakistani boys dance with joy at a blow successfully thrust into the side of an enemy, I realized that they were making an entirely different story out of the pictures from the one I was making. All this made me think, yet again, about the power of stories in human lives . . . the way human beings all tend to make up parts of their own stories, to simplify and edit them, dividing the world into "goodies" and "baddies" (I am using the words we used in the playgrounds of my childhood). Back then, we were always the "goodies"; the "baddies" were other people out there. I sat in the dark, watching those great buildings explode and fall, and thought, automatically, of friends. The boys watched the same thing and thought of enemies.

Then I remembered the Second World War and the dropping of the first atomic bomb on Hiroshima. As a child, this seemed to me and to others around me to be a victory. After all, the Japanese were our enemies. Because of the Japanese, trenches had been dug on the edges of our schoolyard, and we had been made to practice air-raid drills, so that we would know what to do if there was an enemy attack. It was wonderful to think the war was over—wonderful to think the right people had won, even if the dropping of that mysterious new bomb meant that approximately 77,000 people had died. It was only later that the truly alarming nature of the bomb began to give us uneasy feelings—and many people had no uneasy feelings at all. They felt that the Japanese deserved it.

So the World Trade Center has fallen. But, of course, that has not been the end of the matter. Stories have neat endings.

We can shut a story in a book and walk away. But, in real life, things go on and on and on. Within the twenty-four hours that followed the attack, threats were made here in New Zealand against innocent Islamic New Zealanders. Their windows were broken and graffiti was scrawled on their fences. People choose or sometimes invent their own "goodies," their own "baddies." They long for revenge (and I know what that feels like. There have been occasions when I have longed for revenge myself). Edited stories rear up in the world, and of course there is often something of the truth in all these stories, as there is in so many of my own invented tales, but many people are not interested in working their way beyond the story to the complete truth. Often, the complete truth is just too complicated to cope with. So, many people prefer the partial truths of edited versions, which they then declare to be the *whole* truth. And some of those people, like the terrorists who took over the planes, are prepared to defend this partial truth with their lives by killing a lot of innocent and irreplaceable people.

Of course a lot has happened since the twin towers fell. There are New Zealanders who disapprove of the war against the Taliban that the USA (behaving just as we would expect the most powerful nation in the world to behave) has conducted in Afghanistan, and there are other New Zealanders who support it passionately. I know people in the USA feel mixed about what to do next. As I read editorials and articles in newspapers, and letters to the editor in magazines, I can see stories clashing with one another like jostling enemies. Stories leap at us off television screens or stream out of radios; they burrow into us through our eyes and ears. We read print on the page, and the words we are reading, if we invite them in, may knit themselves into our heads and become part of us. Stories had certainly knitted themselves into the lives of those men who piloted the planes that crashed into the World Trade Center towers, and over the last few days I have heard of a fifteen-year-old boy in the USA who stole a plane and crashed it into the side of a tall building somewhere. He must have been trying to make the story come alive all over again and giving himself a leading role in it.

Of course, the story of those terrible attacks on towers at the heart of New York is not over. It is still going on out there . . . not only in New York and Afghanistan but in the heads of many people who saw exactly what I saw on the television screen at two o'clock in the morning. As I write, this news comes at me from the radio (it is 7 A.M. in New Zealand) telling me that prisoners of war in Afghanistan have been badly treated. Some New Zealanders hearing this news will be alarmed (as I am). Others will say that it serves them right. Those prisoners of war are the enemy. They deserve whatever is happening to them.

The radio talks on. I hear that experts are arguing about the laws governing the treatment of prisoners and, at the same time, are explaining how necessary it is to control them. Both things may be true. I find myself recalling that when my daughter (married to that man from Vermont) was a journalist she was told that she must not simply pass on information . . . she must look for the story inside the information, and tell the story, which often involves editing, emphasizing, and eliding. Storytellers play games with ideas and words all the time.

It is a dangerous world but it is wonderful, too . . . happy and hopeful for many of us. Well, I am certainly hopeful a lot of the time and the reading and writing of stories are two of the things that make me happy. But I never forget just how dangerous stories can be when the simple truth of the story is made to stand for the complicated truth of the everyday world. Story truth and world truth both have important parts to play in our lives, but they work differently. In the everyday life we have to struggle toward truth. There is no end to the struggle and it is very tiring, and yet we must never give in. We must never allow the difficult truths of real life to be replaced by the simpler truths of the story.

ABOUT THE CONTRIBUTORS

ARNOLD ADOFF has published more than thirty books of poetry and "poet's prose" for young readers and their "older allies." His style of "shaped speech" is an ordered balance of the meaning and music of language. One of his most interesting titles is a collection of his young adult poems called *Slow Dance Heart-Break Blues*.

JAIME ADOFF's first collection of poems for young readers, *The Song Shoots Out Of My Mouth*, a celebration of music, will be published in the fall of 2002 by Dutton Children's Books. His years as a singer/songwriter and performer helped to shape his original and rhythmic style of poetry. Jaime is the son of Virginia Hamilton and Arnold Adoff. This is the first time he and his father have appeared in the same publication.

MARC ARONSON is an editor and author who has always been interested in placing American history and experience in a global context. He is the author of *Sir Walter Ralegh and the Quest for El Dorado*, winner of the first Robert F. Sibert award and the Boston Globe–Horn Book Award, both in the category of nonfiction; *Art Attack: A Short Cultural History of the Avant Garde*, a New York Times Notable Book; and *Exploding the Myths: The Truth about Teenagers and Reading* (Scarecrow, 2001).

AVI is an amazingly versatile author whose many books include contemporary novels, fantasy, mystery, and historical fiction. Two of his novels—*The True Confessions of Charlotte Doyle* and *Nothing But the Truth*—are Newbery Honor Books, while his novel *Poppy*, the first title in his Dimwood Forest series, won the Boston Globe–Horn Book Award.

JOAN BAUER is a novelist and short story writer. She won a Newbery Honor for her novel *Hope Was Here* and also won the first Los Angeles Times Book Prize in the young adult fiction category for *Rules of the Road*, which also won the Golden Kite Award. A former journalist and screenwriter, she lives with her husband in Brooklyn and writes in a room that overlooks the former site of the World Trade Center.

MARION DANE BAUER is the author of more than thirty books for young people. She has won numerous awards, including a Newbery Honor award for her novel *On My Honor* and the Kerlan Award from the University of Minnesota for the body of her work. A writing teacher as well as a writer, she is on the faculty at Vermont College for the Master of Fine Arts in Writing for Children. Her books have been translated into more than a dozen different languages.

MARINA BUDHOS writes fiction and nonfiction for adults as well as younger readers, often concentrating on the intermingling of cultures. The winner of awards from the Rona Jaffe foundation and the *Kenyon Review*, she served as a Fulbright lecturer in India. Her works include *The Professor of Light; Remix: Conversations with Immigrant Teenagers;* and a recent two-part essay on what people of Indian background think of the popularity of yoga in the West. An extended essay of hers written in response to the 9/11 attacks was featured on the Indian Web site *Tehelka.com.*

MICHAEL CART is a former library director and a past president of the Young Adult Library Services Association. Now a writer, critic, editor, and columnist, he teaches at UCLA and Texas Woman's University. His young adult novel *My Father's Scar* and his anthologies *Tomorrowland* and *Love and Sex* were all selected by the American Library Association as Best Books for Young Adults.

SUSAN COOPER is an English-born writer best known for the five books in her fantasy sequence, The Dark Is Rising, one of which won the Newbery Medal. She has also written TV screenplays that gained two Emmy nominations, and with her husband, the actor Hume Cronyn, she wrote *Foxfire*, a play that ran for seven months on Broadway. She has two children and lives in New York and Connecticut.

SHARON CREECH lived and taught writing in Europe for eighteen years. She has written two picture books—*Fishing in the Air* and *A Fine, Fine School*—and seven celebrated novels for young readers. She won the Newbery Medal for *Walk Two Moons* and a Newbery Honor Award for *The Wanderer*, while *Chasing Redbird* was short-listed for England's Whitbread Award. Her latest novel is *Love That Dog*.

RUSSELL FREEDMAN, one of America's most distinguished writers of informational books for young readers and a pioneer in the innovative use of graphics and photography, won the Newbery Medal for his *Lincoln: A Photobiography* and Newbery Honors for *Eleanor Roosevelt: A Life of Discovery* and *The Wright Brothers: How They Invented the Airplane*. He lives in New York City.

JAMES CROSS GIBLIN has had two distinguished careers: first, as an editor-publisher and now as an acclaimed author of informational books for children and young adults. Among the many awards and prizes he has won are the American Book Award, three Golden Kite Awards, and two Orbis Pictus Honors. His titles include *The Amazing Life of Benjamin Franklin* and *When Plague Strikes: The Black Death, Smallpox, and AIDS*. His newest book is *The Life and Death of Adolf Hitler*. He lives in New York City.

NIKKI GIOVANNI is a distinguished American poet and professor of English and black studies at Virginia Polytechnic Institute and State University. Her many honors include the NAACP Image Award for Literature and the Langston Hughes Award for Distinguished Contributions to Arts and Letters. Her books for young readers include *Grandmothers; Shimmy, Shimmy Like My Sister Kate; The Genie in the Jar; Spin a Soft Black Song*, and others.

BETSY HEARNE is a professor in the Graduate School of Library and Information Science at the University of Illinois, Urbana-Champaign, where she has been the recipient of a University Scholar Award. She is the author of numerous articles and books, including *Choosing Books for Children* and *Beauties and Beasts*, and several novels for children, including *Listening for Leroy* and *Wishes, Kisses, and Pigs*. She won the Jane Addams Children's Book Award for her picture book *Seven Brave Women*. As former children's book editor of *Booklist* and *The Bulletin of the Center for Children's Books*, she has reviewed books for thirty years and contributes regularly to the *New York Times Book Review.*

MARGARET MAHY, a former children's librarian, was born in New Zealand in 1936 and, though she has talked to school classes in many countries, including the USA, has remained a dedicated New Zealander. She is a prolific and acclaimed author of about 200 books for young readers of all ages. Her work commands a huge international readership. She is a two-time winner of the Carnegie Medal—for her novels *The Haunting* and *The Changeover*—and a third novel, *Memory*, was a runner-up. She is also a six-time winner of the New Zealand Library Association's Esther Glen Award and has been named to the Order of New Zealand.

KYOKO MORI was born and grew up in Kobe, Japan, but has lived in the United States for twenty-four years and has taught at St. Norbert College and Harvard University. She is the author of two novels, *Shizuko's Daughter* and *One Bird*, both of which were selected by the American Library Association as Best Books for Young Adults. She is also the author of the adult memoir *The Dream of Water.*

JIM MURPHY is one of America's foremost writers of informational books for young readers. A former editor, he has been a full-time writer since 1977. *The Great Fire* won a Newbery Honor Award and the prestigious Orbis Pictus Award, presented by the National Council of Teachers of English for outstanding nonfiction. *Blizzard!* was a Sibert Award Honor Book.

WALTER DEAN MYERS, who began his career as an editor, is a prolific author of fiction and nonfiction for children and young adults. One of America's most honored authors, he is a five-time winner of the Coretta Scott King Award and recipient of the American Library Association's Margaret A. Edwards Award for lifetime achievement in young adult literature. His novel *Monster* was a National Book Award finalist and winner of the first Michael L. Printz Award, the most important prize in young adult literature. His latest book is the memoir *Bad Boy*.

NAOMI SHIHAB NYE is an Arab American poet, novelist, and anthologist. The recipient of a Guggenheim Fellowship, she has been a visiting writer-in-the-schools since 1974. Her books include the novel *Habibi* and the picture book *Sitti's Secrets*, both of which won the Jane Addams Children's Book Award. Among her anthologies are *What Have You Lost?* and *Salting the Ocean*.

DAVID PATERSON, a self-described "stay-at-home father of two and proud member of the Manhasset fire department," is also a playwright. His adaptation of his mother Katherine Paterson's novel *The Great Gilly Hopkins* was produced by Louisville's Stage One Theater and played at New York's New Victory Theater in 1998. It was praised by *New York Times* critic Lawrence Van Gelder as "an excellent, bittersweet play."

KATHERINE PATERSON, the acclaimed author of more than twenty-five books for young readers, is a two-time winner of both the Newbery Medal and the National Book Award. Her books have been published in twenty-two languages and she is one of only five American writers to receive the most prestigious international award in children's literature, the Hans Christian Andersen Award.

CHRIS RASCHKA is an artist, writer, and musician. His picture books like *Charlie Parker Played Be Bop* and *Mysterious Thelonius* are noted for their innovative fusion of music and image, while others of his books—like the Caldecott Honor Book *Yo? Yes!* and *Waffle*—sensitively explore the emotional needs of young children. He is also the illustrator of Sharon Creech's *Fishing in the Air* and Nikki Giovanni's *The Genie in the Jar.*

SONYA SONES studied with the celebrated poet and teacher Myra Cohn Livingston. Her first book, the novel in verse *Stop Pretending: What Happened When My Big Sister Went Crazy*, won the Christopher Award, the

Claudia Lewis Poetry Award, and the Myra Cohn Livingston Award for Poetry, and was a finalist for the Los Angeles Times Book Prize. Her second novel in verse is called *What My Mother Doesn't Know.* Both books were Best Books for Young Adults and Top Ten Quick Picks for Reluctant Young Adult Readers.

SUZANNE FISHER STAPLES, who worked for many years as a UPI foreign correspondent in Hong Kong, Pakistan, and India, is the author of four books for young readers, including *Haveli, Dangerous Skies,* and *Shabanu: Daughter of the Wind.* All three of these books were selected as ALA Best Books for Young Adults, while *Shabanu* was also a Newbery Honor–winning title. Her most recent book is *Shiva's Fire.*

VIRGINIA EUWER WOLFF, a teacher and violinist, is known as a venturesome, innovative, and critically applauded writer, whose novels include *Probably Still Nick Swansen, The Mozart Season, Bat Six,* and *Make Lemonade,* a Booklist Top of the List Choice. Most recently, *True Believer* won the National Book Award and a Michael L. Printz Honor Award.

Oct. 2002

911

THE BOOK OF HELP